Chosen

"*Chosen for Charlie* celebrates the joy-filled destiny to be on mission for God as a parent. With Jen's thoughtful, provocative, and insightful reflections on the specific calling of the special needs of each child, you will be encouraged to find fresh hope in your personal journey."
                    —**Sue Detweiler**, author, radio host, and pastor at
                                                Life Bridge Church

"This is more than a wonderfully touching and profoundly inspiring memoir, though it is certainly that in spades. It is also theologically and spiritually challenging. This moving book is for all those on a 'special' journey. In fact, I highly recommend it to everyone willing to move to higher ground."
                    —**Dr. Mark Rutland**, president of Global Servants and
                              The National Institute of Christian Leadership

"Jen Forsthoff has given us a most compelling, compassionate, and transparent insight into her incredible journey of faith, doubts, and questions about facing difficult and confusing assignments. This book is a God-given gift that speaks to the heart! I could not stop reading *Chosen for Charlie*, and neither will you!"
                    —**Kemp Holden**, chairman, Worldwide Evangelism

"In *Chosen for Charlie*, Jen beautifully unwraps the gift of what it means to be hand-selected by God to care for a special-needs child. While exposing the raw realities and tender truths of her own story, Jen's biblical and hope-filled teachings continually point back to the Lord as the source of strength for every parent's journey. *Chosen for Charlie* is a tremendous resource for every parent, grandparent, or anyone chosen to love and care for a special-needs child."

—**Becky Thompson**, author of *Hope Unfolding* and *Love Unending*, creator of Scissortail SILK

"There is no more powerful confidence builder in the world than to be 'chosen.' It sets you apart for something significant by someone that really matters. Jen has honestly shared her beautiful heart story so that you, too, may believe in the privilege you have as a 'chosen one.'"

—**Tammy Dunahoo**, vice president of U.S. Operations and general supervisor, The Foursquare Church

"I believe *Chosen for Charlie* will inspire and help you find healing and grace. Seeing the way Jen and her husband lead as parents with such grace and joy is a testimony of God's faithfulness. Get ready to be wrecked in a beautiful way to experience God's healing power through Jen's message."

—**Paul Daughtery**, senior pastor, Victory Church, Tulsa, Oklahoma

Taylor, love you and so grateful for you! Thank you for all your support with this book! It looks beautiful because of you! Sincerely, Jen

Chosen

for Charlie

When God Gifts You
with a Special-Needs Child

Jen Forsthoff

Psalm 138:8

Life Bridge Press

Life Bridge Press

Chosen for Charlie
© 2016 by Jen Forsthoff

These books are available at special discounts when purchased in quantity for use as premiums, promotions, fundraising, and educational use. For inquiries and details, contact: info@suedetweiler.com.

Published by Life Bridge Press LLC, a division of Detweiler LLC
ISBN TPB: 978-1-943613-97-7
ISBN eBook: 978-1-943613-98-4

Cover Photography by Taylor Jennings
Cover Design by Genesis Kohler
Editing and Production by My Writers' Connection (mywritersconnection.com)

To my husband:
the amazing father of our children,
who loves me and leads me into God's destiny

Contents

Foreword

John dashed into the delivery room, in his camouflage garb, with green paint all over his face, just as Nathan's head was crowning. He caught all of us off guard with an unexpected entrance into the world six weeks early and a surprise diagnosis of Down syndrome.

Down syndrome. Just the mention of the word stirs something deep within our hearts and minds.

My thoughts and feelings today, twenty-four years after Nathan's arrival, are wildly different from the beginning of our relationship. I spent that night alone in my hospital room, listening to happy families around me celebrating their babies. My little boy wasn't in my arms. He was in some sterile room under impersonal fluorescent lights, with a catheter in his heart, fighting for his life. As hot tears rolled down my cheeks, I remember whispering into the night, "God, what is this? A bad joke? Well, I'm not laughing!"

After Nathan's shocking, traumatic entry, I didn't know how to process the words chromosomal "mistake." In the quietness of the hospital room, I found myself secretly wondering if God had made a mistake, giving me a baby with special needs. I didn't feel capable of raising a son with Down syndrome. I wasn't prepared for the task, and it wasn't a path I had chosen.

My friend, Jen, more quickly embraced the reality that she was *Chosen for Charlie*, and she graciously invites you into the private world of her joys, challenges, and faith in God during the journey. She has so many wonderful surprises ahead of her on the path.

We had the joy of sharing sixteen years with Nathan before he left us for heaven after being hit by a car. I never imagined we would have to say goodbye so soon. The pain of losing Nathan is beyond words. Little by little, God is healing our hearts, and orchestrating our way through the grief.

Down Syndrome. Just the mention of the word stirs something deep within our hearts and minds.

One thing is certain. Who I am now and who I was when Nathan was born are miles apart.

Today, I see the world through a new set of eyes. Nathan Charles Vredevelt, took me into his heart and changed me forever. More than anyone else, Nathan taught me about my inner self—to embrace both the light and the shadows, to accept my own strengths and weaknesses, to grow beyond my prejudices and judgments, and to be real with myself and others. It was the way Nathan lived. He absolutely insisted, in both refreshing and aggravating ways, on being himself. Pretense was impossible. "What you see is what you get," fit him like a glove.

There is a secret power to this kind of authenticity. It breathes freedom. Nathan's freedom "to be," ignited an energy within me to become more free "to be." This growth didn't come without intense inner struggle. But with the pain came the gain. When we embrace our own weaknesses, we move closer towards loving ourselves and, therefore, loving others like God loves us. Is this not an end for which we were all created?

Nathan also changed my connection with God. During our years together, my interactions with God shifted from the brain to the heart, from the letter to the Spirit, and from the written Word to deeper companionship with the Person of the Word. That doesn't mean I don't use my brain or exercise spiritual disciplines. I do. But there's a new and greater rhythm of unforced grace, spontaneity, and tender two-way conversations with God than before.

Nathan also taught me to appreciate and glean wisdom from those who don't fit social norms. We live in a society that values beauty, bucks, and brains. How does this work for a girl or boy who is born with physical and mental weaknesses? In a culture of competition and power, those like Jen, who are raising children with special needs, have the grand privilege of embracing a different set of values born of God.

I'd like to close my thoughts with a little note to Charlie, and by extension, to all the other precious Charlies and Nathans in the world:

Dear Charlie,

Your originality and sacred story is written and signed by God. You are a rare treasure, created in God's image, called to be a person no one else can be and to do what no one else can do like you in this world. Hold your head high, stand strong in your God-given purpose, and keep on shining God's love through your smiling eyes, regardless of what others say or do. Always remember, you matter!

With my love,
Pam

Pam Vredevelt (pamvredevelt.com) is a licensed professional counselor and best-selling author, *Empty Arms: Hope and Support for Those Who Have Suffered Miscarriage, Stillbirth, or Tubal Pregnancy*. Pam writes about Nathan's angel sightings and true stories of children with special needs who experience encounters with God in *Angel Behind the Rocking Chair: Stories of Hope in Unexpected Places*.

Introduction

It was love at first sight. After thirty-eight weeks, I finally held my firstborn. My beautiful Charlotte Joy. "Charlie," as we would call her, lay on my chest and wriggled under the bright hospital room light. Not knowing how to comfort her, I held her the best I could. Her sweet cry was music to my ears; to finally hear her voice and see her face was more than I could bear. Though nurses buzzed about the room, cleaning and prepping for Charlie's first bath and such things, for those initial moments, the world seemed to shrink to just the three of us.

My husband and I stared at her blinking blue eyes, the tuft of strawberry blonde hair atop her head, her tiny shriveled hands, her precious little body. "We've been waiting for you," I cried. I couldn't look away from her precious face. "Momma loves you so much."

As new parents, we knew we had much to learn. But with soaring hopes of a bright future, we felt sure that, together, we could conquer whatever might come our way.

Just a few days later, we received the phone call that confirmed the doctors' suspicions: Charlie had Trisomy-21. This genetic abnormality, commonly referred to as Down syndrome, was something we never imagined for our family. We knew, of course, that parenting would be a challenge. But parenting a special-needs child, who could possibly be ready for that?

We Are Chosen

I don't think any parent can ever be prepared for that phone call or those test results. If you've heard those words of finality, you know they set you on a path you might never have chosen for yourself. And although you may never have chosen it for yourself, or for your child, I have come to believe that you have, in fact, been chosen by God; He chose you specifically to be the parent for your child.

Since before time began, your child has been a part of God's plan for your life. The test results didn't surprise God. He didn't worry when the doctors expressed their initial concerns. God was not taken aback that you are the parent of a child with special needs. In fact, God has had something special in mind for your life—and mine—all along.

And just as your child is a part of God's plan for your life, you have also been chosen to be a part of your child's life. In God's great design, He has chosen you, He has chosen me, out of everyone else in the world, to be a part of this precious child's life.

We knew, of course, that parenting would be a challenge. But parenting a special-needs child, who could possibly be ready for that?

Viewed this way, we are the lucky ones. We are the ones who are blessed to be given such a precious opportunity. From this perspective, we can view this new life for what it is: a priceless gift.

Why This Book

But I'll be honest. I didn't feel "chosen" when I first heard our daughter's diagnosis. Instead, sad and afraid, I initially turned to anything I could get my hands on that could teach me about this disability. I searched for information on how to best parent our precious Charlie. I found endless information in books and articles, most of which left me more fearful.

In the midst of reading of all that could go wrong in my daughter's body, I found a few personal testimonies of families facing our same situation, stories that stirred hope. But I didn't find anything that gave me a God-centered foundation based on scripture that could help pave a path for parenting a special-needs child. I needed something to help guide my faith through this journey. Out of the need I faced years ago, I bring this book to you.

Though my daughter is only a few months shy of turning four years old, I can tell you that God has already graciously and specifically ministered to our hearts in every season we have faced thus far. And I simply can't keep the hope and strength He has given us to myself.

Oh, I know I still have a long journey ahead. And I know I will make mistakes and learn the hard way. Some days will be wins and others will call for do-overs. I want to share what God has already done—what He is doing. I want to offer you the kind of resource that I longed for back when our journey began.

Embrace the Calling

Parenting a special-needs child is more than a task, more than an assignment, and even more than a marathon filled with challenges and victories. It's a calling to embrace. Although we may—and most likely will—experience stages of confusion, grief, and fear, I believe God will equip us to parent and lead our children into the full life He has for them. As we look to God's Word (the Bible) to guide our understanding and viewpoint, we can learn how to embrace this gift and use it to renew the hope of all that God can do as we trust in Him.

God can and will do so much within and through you and your child. He will perform miracles, show His power, and shine His light through you each day as you allow Him to do so. When things don't make sense, that's when we have to lean on the truth that God is in control. He is! We can trust in His plan and we can trust in His love for us to help us run the race before us.

You Are Not Alone

While writing this book, I have prayed for you. My prayer is that what you read will encourage and strengthen you. Likewise, I hope you are comforted by knowing you are not alone. You are not alone because the Lord is with you, just as He is with me. We serve a good God who never leaves us, whether we are in a valley of trouble or on the mountain top enjoying the view. He is always near, always good, always faithful.

But I also want you to know that you are not alone in your uncertainty, your fears, your frailty, your tears, your anger, or your questioning. Although you may not have a fellow parent in your immediate circle who has walked in your shoes and can relate to your situation, I pray that through this book, you find comfort and hope as I share openly and honestly from my heart. Through this book, we are on this journey together.

My greatest desire is that through the stories and truths I share here, you will see how God can help you thrive as you parent your special-needs child. Whether you are new to these circumstances or many years into this journey, please know that you are not the first to face the calling to raise a child with special needs.

That's right, you are called. You are *chosen* to be your child's parent. And I believe that God does not call us without equipping us with all we need to succeed. God desires that we face this calling while standing on the truth of His Word. He wants us to thrive as we raise our children and lead our families to walk in victory because our lives can be living examples of His goodness and grace!

1
Our Story

And we know that in all things God works for the good of those who love him, who have been called according to his purpose.
—Romans 8:28 (NIV)

We all have a story to tell. I'm not just talking about a story of your summer vacation, or the time you went to the movies and spilled your popcorn, or the story about running late for your doctor's appointment. I am talking about the story each of us has, the one that forever altered our destinies.

Most of us have stories of moments that changed our perspectives on life and gave us new reasons to wake up each morning. One of my stories, for example, is about the moment during my freshman year of college when I saw my future husband. I was talking with a friend on campus, when suddenly my eyes fell on the most handsome boy I had ever seen. He was warming up for an intramural football game. As he threw the ball and ran across the field, I thought to myself, Is this what college boys look like? Cheesy, right? Sounds like the script for an all-too-predictable teenage movie. I feel silly even sharing that now, but as an eighteen-year-old girl, my thoughts were pretty straightforward. Yes it was, absolutely, love at first sight. Our first conversation didn't happen until weeks later, but eventually I got over my shyness, and now, nearly eight years of marriage, two children, and a dog later, that handsome man sits across the dinner table from me each night. The story of when we first met has forever changed my life!

Another story that shaped my life—one that tops all my other stories—is the story of when I met Jesus. I was twelve years old and had no idea that this night was going to forever mark my heart. I remember sitting in a darkened church with my family that day, watching a production about what Christ did for us when He died on a cross. As each scene unfolded before my eyes, I understood—in a new way—that Christ went to the cross to pay the ultimate penalty for my sins, so that I could have eternal life in Him. I had no idea that this night was going to forever mark my heart, but as I watched the display of Christ on the cross, paying the ultimate penalty for my sins so that I might have eternal life in Him, something sparked in me, something clicked. I was flooded with the desire to know Him more.

When the pastor closed the program, he gave the audience the opportunity to respond. I ran to the front of the stage and eagerly waited for the pastor to pray with me. With everything in me, I wanted to say *yes* to Jesus and give my whole life to Him. I had prayed a similar prayer when I was six-years-old. That was a special time I shared with my parents, but in this moment, I had revelation like never before: Christ loved me. He gave His life as a sacrifice so I could know Him. This story is the most precious story I will ever tell.

How Our Journey Began

Chosen for Charlie began with another life-changing story. Whether I am sharing with a friend, acquaintance, or with a fellow mother of a child with Down syndrome, I am always asked the simple question, "Did you know?" They all want to know how I learned that Charlie has Down syndrome. Hearing this story, they better understand who I am as a mother and they also understand a little more about the journey on which the Lord is leading me. So let me share my story with you.

After four years of marriage, my husband and I were ready to start our family. We had our home in order, our finances ready, and our hearts swelled each time we imagined holding a little bundle of joy in our arms. We knew the time was right because we felt ready. We also knew the time was right because we got pregnant right away. My husband and I joke that all it took was a conversation about getting pregnant, and there we were with a pregnancy test showing the undeniable words that I so love: "PREGNANT."

We found out we were pregnant with Charlotte just before Christmas. To share the big news, I wore a custom-made shirt with the words "Early Christmas Present" perfectly stretched across my belly. Our parents were overjoyed. We all celebrated that Christmas, full of excitement and anticipation for our baby's arrival nine months later.

Our prenatal visits were routine and typical in every way. Each visit to the doctor was simple, yet exciting. And as the months passed and the due date grew closer, I grew bigger and bigger.

But everything changed when one of our routine check-ups had not-so-routine results. During an ultrasound, I was lying on the table with my eyes locked on the monitor as the technician slid the device over my belly. She checked each organ and took each measurement. And then, she paused. She measured, re-measured, and re-measured one more time. Our baby had shorter arm and leg bones than expected for this point in my pregnancy. The ultrasound technician quickly directed me to the maternal medicine area of the hospital. Honestly, at this point, not one concern entered my mind. This was our first child, and I didn't know that visits to this area of the hospital were not standard. I thought to myself, *I have shorter legs so I must have passed it along to my baby. She must be taking after her momma.* I didn't expect much of anything out of the ordinary. Boy, was I wrong.

Soon, I sat across from a doctor who discussed the ultrasound findings with me and then asked, "Do you know much about Down syndrome?" *Do I know much about Down syndrome?* Images of a boy with

Down syndrome from my high school came to mind, and pictures I had seen from my genetics book from junior year. Outside of that, I wasn't able to fill in the blanks at all. I quickly replied, "Somewhat…" *Why was he asking me if I knew about Down syndrome?*

He handed me a booklet with illustrations of chromosomes and began to tell me the details of this genetic disorder. I can't remember much of anything he said after his initial question. I looked across the white, printed pages with pictures of all the groupings of chromosomes, each perfectly paired except for the twenty-first pair, which was a unique set of three.

I walked out of the hospital and to my car in a daze. I didn't know what to think or how to respond to the news. I didn't know if I should call my husband or simply let what had just happened sink in. My survival instinct kicked in. So what did I do as soon as I sat in my car and shut the door? I prayed and I cried.

How could this be? What did I do wrong? Have I not been taking care of myself? Is there something wrong with me or my husband? Do I even let my mind go there? Do I pray and have faith that our baby will be totally healthy? Do I tell my family? Will they worry? What if the baby is totally healthy and I get worried over nothing? What am I supposed to feel? What do I do now?

Some mothers find out about their child's diagnosis before they deliver, some after. Regardless of the timing of that discovery, I want you to know that, in the moment, there is no right or wrong way to feel. Some mothers feel guilt, some feel anger, some feel despair, while others feel completely numb. All of those emotions are valid. Remember this too: The emotions you experience in that moment don't matter. So please, don't feel guilty if you felt dread, or anger, or any other confusing emotion when you first learned of your child's diagnosis. What matters are the choices you make in the moments, days, months, and years that follow.

In the initial visit when the possibility of Down syndrome was discussed, the doctor offered the option of further testing, which I declined. Every mother is different, but I had heard stories of false positives as well as possible dangers for the fetus. So I opted for no tests, which meant waiting. Waiting for months, to see if our daughter would be born healthy or with a life-altering disability. Waiting for months, trying to "take every thought captive,"[1] so that fear and worry of the unknown

What am I supposed to feel? What do I do now?

take away the joy of expecting a child. Waiting for months, praying and having conversations with my husband about whether we should share with our family the possibility that our child would be different.

In the months to follow, we opted for ultrasounds every three weeks to continue to monitor our little girl's progress. We chose the name Charlotte Joy, praying and believing that regardless of her diagnosis, she would be a strong little woman filled with joy.

We chose to tell our parents and a few others about the possibility of Down syndrome so they could pray for a healthy baby as well. The unknown was so difficult. We weren't sure if we needed to prepare and plan for a special-needs child or if she would be totally healthy and any worry would be for nothing. We prayed, and prayed, and prayed. That was all we could do and with every ounce of faith we could muster, we believed God would give us a healthy baby—no issues, no concerns, no abnormalities.

August tenth, week thirty-eight came, and baby Charlotte made her debut. After an eleven-hour labor, the nurse laid her on my chest. Looking at her sweet, precious face, I felt completely awed with love for this

---

1   2 Corinthians 10:5

little person who had lived in my belly for all those months. I looked into her blue eyes and cried as I said, "We've been waiting for you! You are so beautiful! Momma loves you." My husband and I cried, overwhelmed with the realization that we were officially parents.

Just moments after her birth, I turned to the doctor and asked, "Is she okay?"

The doctor replied, "Yes, she is totally healthy."

Relief welled up instantly. After months of prayer and the unknown, we had a healthy baby. We rejoiced and couldn't believe how beautiful she was.

But as baby Charlotte and I were recovering in the hospital, our little girl's status quickly changed. The pediatrician came in for Charlie's initial check-up. He looked her over, head to toe, listening to her heart, checking her reflexes, examining every tiny feature. After completing the exam, he left the room only to come back a few minutes later. He wanted to talk. He and another doctor were divided over some features; her lower set ears, the large space between her first and second toe, her almond-shaped eyes, and her struggle to nurse. They said that they needed to do a blood test to be certain; a blood test for Down syndrome. The relief we felt when she was born immediately vanished. We were back to the unknown. So what did we do? We prayed. We prayed. We prayed.

I will never forget when my husband took the call on his cell phone in our bedroom two days later. The results were in. I had followed him up the stairs with Charlie in my arms. He was listening intently to the pediatrician and then his face fell. I knew the answer, but I had to ask, "Does she have it?" I whispered.

He nodded.

My mind went blank. My heart sank. I felt as if the life had been sucked out of me. A heaviness overtook me in a way I had never experienced before. My legs gave way and I fell into my husband's arms. He led me to the bed and gently cradled Charlie and me in his lap.

I needed only one thing—for God to speak.

2
Chosen for Charlie

And who knows but that you have come to your royal position
for such a time as this.
—Esther 4:14 (NIV)

There are times in our lives when we are facing such a storm, such a valley, such a heaviness, that nothing can abate the fear and sorrow we feel. No one can say anything that can change those emotions. When I heard Charlie's diagnosis of Down syndrome, I didn't know what to do or to whom I could turn. My husband and I talked, but we couldn't offer much hope to one another. We were both just trying to keep our heads above water. I reached out to my family. And while I clung to their heartfelt prayers and kind words, I needed something more.

I thought knowledge would be my lifeline, so I dove into books and articles. I researched the diagnosis online, trying to understand what it meant. I thought that if Charlie's medical condition was something I better understood, maybe I wouldn't feel as if I were drowning. I was wrong. The further I researched and read about what other families were experiencing, the more discouraged I became. I would find myself studying the health risks and probability of pains that no child should ever experience and became choked with fear. What if Charlotte's thyroid failed? What if she had to have heart surgery? What if she gets leukemia? My quest for information and understanding only caused my heart to sink even deeper. Don't get me wrong, educating yourself as a parent is important when it comes to helping our children thrive, but at this point, it wasn't helping me—not one bit.

My mother knew a woman who had raised a son with Downs and was willing to talk with me on the phone if I needed someone. I remember lying on my bed and dialing her phone number. A gentle voice answered. I introduced myself and thanked her for offering to speak with me. Unable to stop myself, I poured out my heart to a woman I had never met, but in those moments, I felt closer to her than anyone I had ever known. For the first time since all this had begun, I connected with another mother who knew exactly what I was experiencing. She understood what it was like to feel all the same confusion and wash of emotions. Our conversation was a life-giving breath that lifted a great deal of my heaviness. Even so, I needed something more.

Then God Spoke

As a new mother, one of my daily goals was to make the time to bathe myself once a day. Isn't it funny how such a simple task can seem almost impossible when caring for a newborn? For me, the shower was a place of solitude, a place where I could be alone with God. One day, when Charlie was only a few weeks old, I stood in the shower feeling totally and completely numb. As the water washed over me, I felt a simultaneous sensation of heaviness and emptiness. "God, I need you to speak," I whispered. A simple prayer, but an honest one. I couldn't utter anything else. Fortunately, I didn't need to.

Have you ever felt as if you have come to the end of yourself—totally depleted and desperate? That's exactly how I felt. And I knew that, unless God intervened—unless He spoke to my heart—the heaviness I felt would drown me.

I needed God to say something. As good as my husband, my family, or even another mother who had been in my shoes could be in this season, their words couldn't comfort me.

There, my desperate plea spoken into the steam, I heard God speak: "I chose you to be her mom."

A peace came over me. The heaviness and emptiness that had been building left me. His words stirred so sweetly in my spirit. I was chosen to be her mom. Out of all the mothers in the world, *I was chosen to be Charlie's mom. I GET to be her mom.* As I pondered this realization, I felt an overwhelming sense of pride at the honor of being chosen by God to love and care for Charlie. *Since before time began, I have been God's plan for Charlie's life and she has been God's plan for mine. I was chosen for Charlie.* I was.

There, my desperate plea spoken into the steam, I heard God speak: "I chose you to be her mom."

His words to me brought palpable relief. I went from feeling as if I were drowning to feeling a surge of energy—and sincere gratitude—for the gift of being called by God to be this precious baby's mother. There was also a feeling of awe, that God trusted Luke and me with Charlie's abilities and disabilities.

His Plan for Us

In the Old Testament, we read about a time when God needed someone to deliver the children of Israel from the Egyptians and into the Promised Land. God chose Moses. Could some other shepherd who was on the same shift as Moses have been the one to see the burning bush that day? Could it have been a coincidence that Moses just happened to walk by and see those flames?

No.

God chose Moses. In fact, since Moses' birth, God had been pursuing him specifically and purposefully. God had seen every strength, every weakness, every failure, every step Moses had taken up until the moment they met at the burning bush. And even after seeing the good and the bad, Moses was *still* the one God wanted. Because God knew something; He knew He was not just calling Moses to lead the children of Israel, but He Himself would be with him and help him every step of the way.

In this same way, we are chosen for *our* children. Before time began, God designed you for your children—and your children for you. What a privilege and honor to be entrusted with them! While you may worry that someone much more qualified could do a better job than you, keep in mind that God specifically and purposefully gave your son or daughter to you. When we commit ourselves to prayer and seek the Lord for His wisdom and guidance in raising our children, we can be confident that we are the best parents for our child, special needs or not. God knows our personalities, weaknesses, and strengths. He plans good things, designing our families in such a way that it is never an accident, never a mistake, never a curse.

God knows full well whom He is choosing. He does not make mistakes. He never makes a decision on a whim or without full wisdom and omnipotence. In Proverbs 2:6, God is called the source of all wisdom and understanding. While we are limited in knowing and understanding the great plans of God, there is no limit to what He sees and what He orchestrates each moment of each and every day. From Isaiah 55:8, we learn that God's ways are not our ways. He has revealed His love and character, and so we can trust that His ways are *better* than ours! What He chooses and ordains in this life is better than anything we could ever choose or plan for ourselves because He knows and understands how each life will proceed. I'm not saying He makes our choices for us, just that He knows and understands us, and therefore, is able to plan wonderful things for us. When we plan for ourselves, with our limited understanding of what will create the best future for us, we may not even realize the joys we're missing out on.

When I was young, there was a brief period of time when I said I would never marry a pastor. I had grown up as a PK (pastor's kid), and I knew very well the effort that it takes each week to build the Church. It truly is an intense and exhausting labor of love. And over time, I lost that love. Taking care of the Church (the people) and the church (the building) is more than a forty-hour work week. Being the first ones to show up and the last ones to leave week in and week out drained me emotionally and physically. Years of serving as a Sunday school teacher, janitor, worship leader, and kitchen helper led to the inevitable—total and utter burnout. In my youthful enthusiasm, I spread myself too thin. Rather than drawing strength and direction from the Lord, I became a "yes" person and didn't recognize my own limits.

Familiar only with the unhealthy pattern I had created, I wanted to establish myself, my marriage, and my family so that we would simply attend and have no emotional, mental, or physical investment in the local church. Well, wouldn't you know that when I fell in love with Luke, he was studying to become a pastor! Now I praise God that my plans and selfish desires didn't determine my path. God, because He truly knows what will bring delight and satisfaction to me as He accomplishes His will, has led me on a much better journey! Together, my husband and I invest our time, energy, and resources into the work of strengthening and encouraging the Church. Because of God's good, flawless plan, my life and what I get to do for the Lord are above and beyond anything I could ever have imagined.

I know that He has carefully designed a good plan for your life, too. God placed our children in our care because He has a great plan. And that plan will benefit both our children and our own lives because He works all things together for good (Romans 8:28).

Our Gift from God

I know you may be questioning, even struggling with thoughts of whether a child with special needs is really a good plan for your life. And while I once wondered that, too, I can now confidently point you to His Word. In Psalm 127:3 (NLT), it says, "Children are a gift from the Lord." I don't see any qualifiers in that verse. It doesn't say children are a gift from God if they are not diagnosed with a disability. It doesn't say children are a gift from God if they behave just as you want them to. It doesn't say children are a gift from God when everything turns out the way you want. It says children are a gift from God. Period. My Charlie is a gift and so is your child!

Shortly after Charlie's birth, a woman who had recently found out that Charlie had been diagnosed with Down syndrome sat down to talk to me. I was in my initial stages of grief and pain, still processing everything. "I heard about Charlotte," she said softly. "You don't think you are cursed, do you?"

Cursed? Out of all the thoughts that had flooded my mind since we had received the news about our daughter, *cursed* was never one that occurred to me. Maybe you have felt that way about your child, but the truth is that your child, regardless of his or her condition or challenge, is a pure and lovely gift from our heavenly Father (James 1:17).

One of the hardest questions my husband and I asked ourselves was, "Is this our fault?" Does Charlie have this disability because of something I carry genetically, something I did or neglected to do during my pregnancy? I remember tossing and turning for hours one night. I got up to go to the bathroom, and the thought came to me, What if it was my fault that Charlie was born with Down syndrome? There must be something wrong with my body. I didn't make a healthy baby. What is wrong with me? I hate my body! The guilt caused by the belief that I could have prevented or caused Charlie's condition weighed heavily on my heart.

One of the hardest questions my husband and I asked ourselves was, "Is this our fault?"

Luke and I even sought genetic counseling to see if we might be carriers of a genetic abnormality that could have caused our daughter's condition. We wanted to understand why this had happened. We also hoped to have more children and wanted to know if we could avoid the possibility of Down syndrome in any of our future children. The geneticist gave us the same results as all the other studies: It just happened.

There is no known cause or no definitive explanation for why some children are born with Down syndrome. It occurs in 1 in every 792 births. No one knows what causes the third copy of the twenty-first chromosome, despite research and parents who question and wrestle to find the answer.

We may never know the ultimate reason behind Charlotte's DNA. But what I do know is that if we focus on the fight to know the *why*, we will miss out on the *now*. And right *now*, I have a beautiful daughter whom God has entrusted into my care. I have the honor and privilege of raising and loving her. Although current studies don't provide black and white answers for all our questions, I believe a bigger answer can quell our questions and eliminate any guilt. That answer is that God has chosen us.

Take Hold of His Word

The only reason I have this perspective is because God answered my prayer that day in the shower. God spoke and His words changed everything for me. Maybe God has spoken to you about your child and it changed everything for you. If so, I rejoice with you and am so grateful He has revealed His truth to you! Hold onto that word and don't let anyone or anything ever diminish it.

If you feel as I did—filled with heaviness and overcome by the thought of raising the child you have been given—ask God to speak. He may use others to encourage you in powerful ways, but nothing anyone else can say will ever compare to the peace that comes when God, the Creator of the universe, the King of Kings, the Alpha and Omega (which means the Beginning and the End), speaks a word to your heart at just the right moment.

When God speaks to us, it is our responsibility to hold on to what He has said, to commit it to memory and treasure it in our hearts. Just as Mary treasured in her heart what the angel told her about being the mother of Jesus, it's important for us to ponder and treasure what God speaks to us (Luke 2:19). We can "stand" on His Word and rely on it as a firm foundation! Some days I feel like I am failing as a mom because I can't keep up with Charlie's therapy exercises or spend the hours she needs to develop her speech. Some days I don't know the best way to discipline her so that she can fully understand boundaries. Some days our finances and what Charlie needs from doctors and specialists don't add up. On those days, I go back to one thing. I go back to when God spoke. *You are chosen for Charlie.*

In spite of my weaknesses as a parent, I have been entrusted with this precious gift. Because Christ is strong when I am weak, I can push forward in His strength.

*But he said to me, "My grace is sufficient for you, for my power is
made perfect in weakness." Therefore I will boast all the more gladly
about my weaknesses, so that Christ's power may rest on me.*

—2 Corinthians 12:9 (NIV)

In my weaknesses and lack of understanding and even in finances,
God has proven to be strong and to do miraculous things! When I have
felt that all my efforts to help Charlie with her therapy exercises weren't
enough to make the progress happen, that was exactly when she started
to show more coordination than ever! Or when she needed that next pair
of braces that we couldn't afford, God miraculously provided through
another family donating a pair of braces that were the perfect fit for our
daughter. He is good and His love endures forever (1 Chronicles 16:34)!

Perhaps the word that God spoke to me is what He is speaking to
you in this moment. In essence, it's the same word He spoke to Esther
about being placed in a position for such a time as this so that God might
save His chosen people, glorify Himself, and advance His plans here on
earth (Esther 4:14). You have been chosen for your child! Embrace that
honor, hold onto that gift, and let that truth forever shape your perspective about the precious child with whom you have been entrusted. Find
peace in God's Word and know that He will use your child for His glory!

3
For His Glory

"Neither this man nor his parents sinned," said Jesus, "but this happened so
that the works of God might be displayed in him."
—John 9:3 (NIV)

In the Garden of Gethsemane, Jesus came face to face with His destiny. Knowing what awaited Him—moments of betrayal, agony, and pain greater than any could imagine—He went to His Father. While His disciples stayed close by, Jesus prayed.

And going a little farther he fell on his face and prayed, saying,
"My Father, if it be possible, let this cup pass from me; nevertheless,
not as I will, but as you will." And he came to the disciples and found
them sleeping. And he said to Peter, "So, could you not watch with
me one hour? Watch and pray that you may not enter into temptation.
The spirit indeed is willing, but the flesh is weak." Again, for the sec-
ond time, he went away and prayed, "My Father, if this cannot pass
unless I drink it, your will be done." And again he came and found
them sleeping, for their eyes were heavy. So, leaving them again, he
went away and prayed for the third time, saying the same words again.

—Matthew 26: 39-44 (ESV)

Being fully man and fully God, Jesus knew what was before Him and deeply wrestled with His destiny—death on a cross. He knew that the Father had a master plan through the unfolding of His own destiny; His death would bring life to the world. Salvation for all mankind and the promise of the new covenant awaited. The design and the reward of God's plan surpassed the pain of the moment that lay before Him. Jesus wanted the Father's will, even if it meant momentary suffering and pain. He knew that greater victory was promised.

Ask the Hard Questions

When God is speaking to me through the Scriptures, I like to ask myself questions that cause me to look inward and evaluate what is at work in my life. I like to take notes while listening to my pastor preach. I frequently pause and take a moment, not to write the next bullet point, but to write down a question related to the point being illustrated in the sermon. I reflect on the condition of my heart and the perspective that guides my daily life.

When it comes to raising our children, our questions can be endless. We have questions about the future, about their roles in society, about their potential. But beyond these, I have wrestled with a few questions that opened the door for God to work deeply in my heart, questions I was afraid to ask myself and even more afraid to answer.

1. *Is God's glory the most important thing to me?*

2. *Is my life's happiness determined by met expectations or God's glory being fulfilled?*

3. *Would I rather live a comfortable, successful life (in the world's eyes) or allow God to work in and through my family as He sees fit?*

4. *Is this life about my hopes and dreams being fulfilled or God's hopes and dreams being fulfilled?*

5. *Do I want my life spent so that God can be known?*

Dig deeply into your own soul. Asking these questions for yourself may make you a bit squeamish, just as they did me when I first began to really reflect on a passage of scripture that shook the core of who I am. I never thought it wrong to want good things for my family—and it's not. But to desire what makes us happy and comfortable over that which brings God the most glory is.

Different Is the New Normal

I love it when God speaks through His Word! That's why it's so important that we read or listen to it daily so that it feeds our souls. His Word is our daily bread, and through it, God's truth can guide our lives. I also love how the Holy Spirit brings these ancient words to life and makes them fresh and relevant to our current reality.

There is a Bible verse that I read hundreds of times before Charlotte's birth, but when I came across it after her diagnosis, it's meaning seemed completely different. The words hadn't changed, but my heart and perspective had changed drastically. Don't you love it when that happens?

The verse is in John 9, which tells the story of a man who encountered Jesus and His disciples. Born blind, he had never seen his mother's face, never seen the beauty of creation around him, had never even seen his own reflection. Imagine the frustration his parents must have experienced while raising him. I am sure that, as a young boy, he needed constant help getting dressed, feeding himself, moving throughout the city in which he was raised. Perhaps he was rejected by his peers because he was different. It's very likely he couldn't keep up with the rest of the boys his age having foot races through the streets. He probably longed for friends and companions who would look past his disability and accept him for who he was. He may have grown tired of others not believing in him or dismissing his capabilities, simply because he was different.

I imagine his parents celebrating the milestones of independence, so proud to see him become a part of society and in spite of his limitations.

I also imagine them late at night, when their son had gone to bed, over-whelmed with grief and heart ache—another day of frustrations, dead ends, repetition, feeling as though they took one step forward only to take five steps backward. Can you relate? I sure can.

This family only knew this reality. Raising a blind child was their "normal." As parents, they didn't know what it was like to raise him with the luxury of sight. All they knew were the frustrations and challenges of helping their son survive in a world that was designed for people with sight. They also knew that there was no such thing as a small victory for their boy—every moment of overcoming was to be celebrated and marked as another step forward for their son.

In raising a child with special needs, we will never know "normal" as the world describes it. Our "normal" is specialists, therapies, surgeries, and constant personal research so that our child can have every advantage to excel. Though different from others' lives, this is our normal. We can choose to embrace our circumstances, or if we do not choose this, we can be overcome by them. I wonder what the family of this blind son chose.

In raising a child with special needs, we will never know "normal" as the world describes it... We can choose to embrace our circumstances, or if we do not choose this, we can be overcome by them.

Not so long ago, I talked with a friend who also has a daughter with Downs. We laughed at what a trip to the park with our daughters looks like. While some parents may sit on the park bench, sip coffee, and relax in the peaceful morning, our experience is very much the opposite. We are in a constant state of alert and caution to protect our little ones from any eminent danger lingering at every corner. Yes, you are right, I will say it so you don't have to—I am the "helicopter" mom. I am the one who climbs every ladder and follows Charlie around each turn because I imagine the worst-case scenario for my sweet three-year-old. Her weak muscles, lack of balance, and slower reaction time could lead her over the side of the bright, red platform or the edge of a swirly slide. Sure, sipping on a hot coffee would be ideal, but visiting the park is an all-hands-on-deck ordeal. Although tiring at times, I have learned to accept this as a "normal" trip to the park. You may want to tell me to chill out and not be so protective, but that's how we roll at the park and stay alive.

The WHY Factor

Back to the family in John 9. One day, Jesus and His disciples saw this blind man as they were out walking. Perhaps he looked a bit helpless, begging for sympathy and compassion from passersby. The disciples had encountered this type of situation before—someone hurting and needing Jesus to help them, touch them, speak to them.

Noticing the blind man, they wondered why this was his lot, just as many people today still ask the hard questions about suffering in the world and debate the "why" behind difficulties in life. So the disciples asked Jesus, "Rabbi, who sinned, this man or his parents, that he was born blind?" (John 9:2, NIV) The *why* behind our circumstances always seems to trip us up.

When Charlie was born, I so badly wrestled with the why. *Why did this happen? Why us?* I blamed myself for a time. *There must be something wrong with my body,* I thought. *Why can't I make a healthy baby?* I am being vulnerable with you because I believe I am not alone. If we can know the *why*, it gives us something or someone to blame. We crave the reason so that we can channel our emotion, our anger, towards that something or someone.

I mentioned earlier that Luke and I went to a geneticist. We thought a consultation would help bring clarity and something we desperately desired: the answer to why we had a child with a genetic abnormality. Nothing in our family's health history provided clues. And so we wondered and desperately sought answers. *Was it something I carried? Something my husband carried? Why did this happen?* Perhaps you have questioned like we did. Your questions may sound different, but I am sure that you have lost sleep pondering the why behind your child's disability.

After evaluations and lengthy questioning, the answer behind Charlotte's almond-shaped eyes, petite stature, and developmental delays was: *It just happened.* Down syndrome happens at the point of conception. There is no definite cause. There can occasionally be a parent who carries a gene that increases the possibility of a genetic abnormality, but in our case, pure chance. So they say. But after reading John 9, I know it was anything but chance.

Jesus hears the questions, "Was it him or was it his parents? Why was the blind man born this way?" I imagine the man, along with the disciples, eagerly awaiting Jesus' response. He would finally hear the *why* behind his "normal" life. I am sure Jesus' reply shocked the disciples and the blind man.

For His Glory

Jesus replies to the disciples' question, "…this happened so the works of God might be displayed in him" (John 9:3, NIV).

Reading this passage, I had to ask myself, "Do I want God to be glorified or my child to be what the world says is normal? Do I want a glorious life for myself, or do I want God's glory to be revealed here on earth—even at the expense of a comfortable life? If the sleepless nights, the tears cried, the medical expenses, the labels from society, and the rejection from others opens the door for God to do something glorious—will I accept it?"

God will glorify Himself through your child. There will be countless opportunities for God to show Himself as faithful, powerful, and near. For in our weakness, His power is made perfect (2 Corinthians 12:9). God often uses our children to show His love, His goodness, and His grace in the most beautiful way. As we love our children, our testimony is clear to others, pointing them to God Almighty. Although our "normal" has its moments of difficulty, it is that very "normal" that displays the glory of God for all to see!

*God will glorify Himself
through your child.*

Every victory, breakthrough, and good report we get about Charlotte's health and development is a testimony to the goodness of God. As God's healing hand is at work in her life, we share it so that He is glorified. As God provides finances, gives us favor, and continues to bring grace in every season, we have the opportunity to bring Him glory and speak of His wondrous works in our lives!

Every six months, Charlotte gets her blood drawn to check her thyroid. And every test thus far has shown her thyroid to be healthy and functioning properly. And for that, we praise God and give Him the credit! We declare these moments of breakthrough and victories so that His glory can be known. It is through our testimony of Christ and His miracles in our lives that we overcome (Revelation 12:11).

How Will His Glory Be Shown?

In this story of the blind man, Jesus performs a miraculous healing. Using His homemade salve recipe—saliva and dirt—Jesus touches the man's eyes and tells him to wash in the Pool of Siloam. "So the man went and washed and came home seeing" (John 9:7, NIV).

This scripture excites me! I love that the blind man is completely healed. His parents must have been overwhelmed when they saw their son who could now see them for the first time. Seeing each other face—to—face, what a moment of celebration! I want to cry, just thinking of parents seeing their child fully healed!

Yes, I cry out to God, asking that He heal Charlotte miraculously, that He bring wholeness to her mind and body and amaze every doctor and specialist with His healing power. I would love it if God showed His glory in this way!

Is it okay to pray for miraculous healing for our children? I believe so. I know I want to pray the biggest, boldest prayers I can for my children. I don't want to hold back, only to later find out that if I had only prayed for bigger, greater things, then God would have done the impossible. Just as God did when Elijah prayed earnestly for Him to hold off the rain for three years (James 5:17), I want the prayers I pray for my children to change history.

If God totally heals our children, He will be glorified! And if God performs miracles along the way, He will be glorified! Just remember that there is no such thing as a small miracle. All miracles are worth celebrat-

Just remember that there is no such thing as a small miracle.

ing and God is glorified through our testimony of these miracles. When my soul can rest in the will and goodness of the Father, I can trust that He will use our family, and our precious Charlie, for His glory.

Charlie is almost four years old, and I can honestly say that God has, time and time again, already shown His glory in and through her. And as her mother, I pray and believe that God can fully heal her. But if it brings Him more glory to work otherwise, then let it be so. Even when I don't understand His ways or His plans, I believe that they are higher and better than my own. He has been nothing but faithful and good, so I trust that He knew exactly what He was doing when He created Charlie and gave her to our family.

Embrace His Will

God had a design and a plan for us and our children since before time began. Rather than fighting His plans or despising them, let's embrace them so that He can be glorified. In the rough moments, we may not want His glory over our comfort and expectations. But even then, we can trust that God is up to something great. And if we yield to His good plans, He will show Himself, His love, and His glory. God is not a man that He should lie or forsake the goodness of who He is (Numbers 23:19). God is good. God is faithful. God is love.

For the earth will be filled with the knowledge of the glory of the Lord as the waters cover the sea.

—Habakkuk 2:14 (NIV)

4
Life to the Full

*The thief comes only to steal and kill and destroy; I have come that they may
have life, and have it to the full.*
—John 10:10 (NIV)

For a season of my life, I was an elementary school teacher. In this profession, I had the privilege of helping to shape the future of young people. Every student who sat in my classroom had a future full of hope, excitement, and passion.

And each one had a parent.

A parent who helped shape the dream of the young man who imagined his life spent out on the football field, catching touchdown passes, and living the high life of a pro-athlete.

A parent who saw his daughter's great potential, intelligence, and discipline and trusted that those strengths would one day enable her to become a doctor and help save lives.

A parent who encouraged her child's artistic side, believing that every drawing and every painting was a masterpiece and that her talent could help make the world a more beautiful place.

Regardless of the dream or profession we imagine for our children, all the things we parents do for them, our efforts, stem from our desire that they enjoy full and meaningful lives. We want them to have a life of significance, spent with those they love, discovering and running after their unique purposes, and pursuing their passions. We want our kids to have what we have had or what we wished we had. Anything that brought a smile to our face we hope will one day bring a smile to theirs. Our desire is that they will experience the same joyous moments and a fulfilling destiny.

That's why so many parents enthusiastically, and sometimes ridiculously, cheer for their children on the sidelines of the soccer field. We buy the gear, the uniforms, drive to the far-away tryouts and tournaments, all so our children can have the experience we want so badly for them—the thrill of victory and accomplishment.

The experiences we have as a child help shape the adult we become. I have such fond memories of summer camp as a young thirteen-year-old girl—hopping into the car with my best friends for a week-long adventure in the mountains of Colorado. We spent the week hiking, rock climbing, staring at the night sky by a warm, crackling camp fire, performing goofy skits for fellow campers, and of course, chasing boys. Being far from home and loving parents, I occasionally felt homesick and made a tear-filled call to Mom and Dad.

A few years later, I experienced some of the most meaningful times with the Lord while serving on short-term missions, the intensive ministry that occurred during seven power-packed days filled with one-on-one evangelism, prayer, dramas, and corporate worship. Being immersed in a different culture and seeing my awesome, powerful God outside of my everyday life has profoundly shaped my faith and how I view the world around me.

All of those adventures and the emotions that came with them taught me life lessons and made me a little bit more of who I am today. My experiences, the friendships I have made, and my successes and failures have all given me great stories to tell and memories to treasure.

Full Life

In my life, I have experienced the richness of deep relationships. I consider myself very blessed to have friendships that have withstood the tests of time, distance, and obstacles. I have friends who seem more like sisters, with whom I can share my deepest fears and dreams, while knowing I am fully accepted just as I am. Along with friendships, I have the joy of being married to an incredible man of God who loves me and cares for me in a way that I could never deserve. And I know the joy of having children who reach up to have me hold them close, who give goodnight kisses that leave me slobbery and melt my heart, and who, when I hear them call out, "Momma," have me wrapped around their tiny little finger.

I have been blessed to get a degree from a private Christian university that, while educating me and preparing me for the world ahead, also shaped my faith and forever solidified my relationship with my Savior. I worked in incredible schools alongside wise mentor-teachers and administrators who are molding and shaping future generations. I can't think of too many things that are as rewarding as teaching a child to read, to solve problems, and to develop confidence that will help lead them into a bright and hope-filled future.

My life has been very fulfilling thus far. I am so grateful for the work of God in my life and the experiences He has blessed me with.

When I think about my daughter's life, I am not sure how many similar experiences she will have. At the beginning of our journey with Charlie, I wondered so many things. *Will she get to go to summer camp one day? Will she ever go on a mission trip? Will she have best friends like I had? Will she get married? Will she ever experience the joy of being a mother? Will she go to college? Will she ever be independent and have a career?*

I have an intense desire for Charlotte to experience the great things I have experienced. I want her to have the close friendships. I want her to have sleepovers and travel for spring break. I want her to play sports, play the piano, be a part of clubs at school that will help her to belong to a group and instill values and self-esteem. I want her to go on mission trips that will strengthen her faith and show her how powerful, incredible, and steadfast God is.

I want so much for my little Charlie-girl. I want her to finish high school, go to college, get married, and live on her own. Will she do any of those things? Only the Lord knows. I believe that most of these experiences might happen for her to an extent, but surely they will play out differently in her life.

The Truth That Changed Me

I don't want to be a downer, but in all honesty, I have battled over and over with the thoughts of what Charlie may never get to experience. I still occasionally wrestle with these thoughts. But now, when my worries begin to well up, the Holy Spirit reminds me of what Scripture tells me do: talk to the Lord and ask for Him to intervene and show His path.

One ordinary day, when Charlie was two years old and just beginning to walk and jabber, God showed me a passage of Scripture that soothed my worries about Charlie's future. Since the time God spoke this passage to my heart, I have thought differently about her life. While I still think about what she may or may not experience, I no longer worry about the quality of life she will have.

I had heard the verse a thousand times but had never applied it to our family situation with Charlie. It's found in the book of John where Jesus is teaching the Pharisees that He is the Shepherd who will lay down His life for His sheep and has led us into His protection and pasture through salvation.

Jesus says, "I have come that they may have life and have it to the full" (John 10:10, NIV). It is through Jesus and our salvation in Him, that we have life in the safe, green, lush pasture. *Full life comes through knowing Jesus!*

The truth in this scripture transformed my understanding of what a full life truly is. It is not the camps, travels, friendships, and career that

When my worries begin to well up, the Holy Spirit reminds me of what Scripture tells me do: talk to the Lord and ask for Him to intervene and show His path for my daughter and me.

will give Charlie a full and satisfying life; it's Jesus who can do that! Jesus has a full life planned for my daughter, as she knows Him more fully. To know Christ is to know life! When she accepts Christ into her life, she will be flooded with love, joy, and strength that will lead her to have a fulfilling life. Beyond this, maybe she will have similar experiences to mine, but those are simply a bonus. Being in Christ is all she needs. Being in Christ is all I need (Philippians 4:19). Whether she accomplishes much or little, her value and joy will be found in Christ and the salvation He offers. Even if she never graduates high school or gets married, if she loves Jesus and knows His intimate and unfailing love for her, she has everything she needs to live life to the full.

He Is Everything

I imagine we have all heard testimonies of the rich, well-to-do man or woman who seemed to have it all—a beautiful family, enormous home, successful career—but still felt an emptiness that left them unsatisfied. The stories shared by these men and women possess a common theme: the realization that they didn't comprehend what life was all about until they began their relationship with Jesus. Rich or not, famous or obscure, educated or blue collar, we only experience true life when we take hold of the life He paid the price for on the cross.

To fully enjoy the journey you are on with your child, it's important to understand that, even though he or she may beat all odds and accomplish above and beyond what was ever predicted or expected by any doctor or teacher, the only thing that brings true satisfaction and meaning is a close relationship with Jesus.

> *Let them give thanks to the Lord for His lovingkindness, and for His wonders to the sons of men! For He has satisfied the thirsty soul, and the hungry soul He has filled with what is good.*
>
> *—Psalm 107:8-9, (NASB)*

Jesus is everything we need to satisfy our hunger and thirst—for me, for you, and for our children.

So rather than putting my energy into pushing Charlie to have life experiences that I have enjoyed, I pray and strive to lead her to knowing Jesus better. The greatest experience I can dream for my daughter is to be saved by grace through faith in Jesus and what He did on the cross. I can imagine nothing better than her having a thriving relationship with Him. He will satisfy her deepest desires and lead her in His perfect way. He will order her steps and shape the path for the life He desires for her. Psalm 37:23 (NIV) says, "The LORD makes firm the steps of the one who delights in him."

The best thing I can hope for Charlie is that she fulfills not my plans for her life but the Lord's. More than anything else, I need to want Jesus for Charlie. Nothing else will satisfy her. I praise God for this truth and I hope you do, too!

Jump Start

John Knight, director of donor partnerships at Desiring God, has four children, one of which has multiple disabilities, including blindness, autism, cognitive impairments, and a seizure disorder. He wrote an article titled, "The Happiest People In the World," in which he shares these statistics:

- 99 percent of those surveyed are happy with their lives.
- 97 percent answered yes to the question, "Do you like who you are?"
- 99 percent agreed with the statement, "Do you love your family?"

What an incredible finding! Do you know of any group of people, of any economic status, educational level, age, ethnicity, or geographic region who approach those percentages? Who are these happy people? *People living with Down syndrome.*

So rather than putting my energy into pushing Charlie to have life experiences that I have enjoyed, I pray and strive to lead her to knowing Jesus better.

Although they may face hardships due to disabilities and learning complications, "people with Down syndrome report much greater happiness in their lives than any other demographic sample in any part of the world." Those with Down syndrome often seem to enjoy the simple things in life and are not weighed down with the typical pressures and stresses others might experience. And as far as their relationships, they have a genuine love for people and find much satisfaction in sharing and receiving that love. With this in mind, my sweet Charlie already has a better perspective on life and what she expects out of herself, others, and the world around her! So if your child is like mine, he or she already has a jump start on a happy life. If the challenge your child faces is different, I hope these statistics will encourage you to believe that having a special need with hardships and difficulties is not a one-way-ticket to an unhappy, unsatisfying life.

Our Full Lives

As I reflect more on the truth that *in Jesus alone is full life*, I realize something deeper still. It wasn't the sum of the experiences themselves that shaped me and gave me a full life. They were simply a tool in the Father's hand to show me more of Himself and draw me closer to Jesus, the Giver of life. God doesn't need a sports team, a sleepover, or a spring-break trip with friends to give me joy. *He Himself is joy!* I don't need to travel to another country to experience adventure. *He is the adventure!* I don't need children or a spouse to know true love. *He is love!* So perhaps Charlie's life will be filled with fewer distractions and more of the beautiful simplicity of knowing Jesus, loving family, and embracing each day for what it is: a tool in God's hand to help us know Him better.

I want you to understand my heart regarding this matter because I know this can be a subject that parents feel very differently—and *strongly*—about. While raising Charlotte, I have encountered many parents, all of whom have passionate opinions and even deep convictions about what the future holds for their children. Though equally as loving, some parents are satisfied with lowering the standard for their child's behavior, physical development, and cognitive achievements, while others strive for total independence, overcoming odds in every area, and breaking the mold of what has been for children with their disabilities. Some parents don't want to push too hard and drive their children to be something they feel like they simply aren't meant to be. While others ask the hard questions, blaze the new path, and don't let anything get in the way of the potential they see in their son or daughter. Both are motivated by love.

Honestly, I see merit in both perspectives. Both want their children to be happy in life. I know that children with special needs can vary tremendously. Our goals as parents can be very different based on our child's physical and cognitive capacity. In Down syndrome alone, the spectrum is vast. You hear stories of families rarely leaving the hospital. You also hear of those who walked their children down the aisle to get married, supported them in pursuing a career, and watched them become parents. For myself, I want to find balance between the two—the parent who is at peace and the parent who pushes for more.

One of my consistent, heart-felt prayers goes something like this,

Lord, give Luke and me wisdom in raising Charlie and making decisions for her health. Give us favor with doctors, therapists, and teachers. Please put the right people in her path to help her grow and develop into the woman you have called her to be.

I want Charlie to thrive. I will do everything I can as a parent to help her reach her potential. I will not sit back and be apathetic in her development and simply hope for her to advance. But at the same time, I choose not to let the meaning and purpose for her life hang on an event or experience that the world may think makes her life more valuable. She is *fearfully and wonderfully made*, and in Christ, she is a *new creation* and has *everything* she needs (Psalm 139:14, 2 Corinthians 5:17, Philippians 4:19).

May we strive as parents to lead our children to know Christ and the life He has for them through salvation. And the good news is that we don't have to do this on our own. We can take hold of the strength and wisdom given from our Heavenly Father and link arms with our spouse, our family, and those dear friends who are called to this journey with us!

5
Better Together

Two are better than one, because they have a good return for their labor.
If either of them falls down, one can help the other up. But pity the man
who falls and has no one to help them up. Also, if two lie down together,
they will keep warm. But how can one keep warm alone? Though one may
be overpowered, two can defend themselves. A cord of three strands is not
quickly broken.
—Ecclesiastes 4:9-12 (NIV)

Some people, when faced with challenges in life, internalize the issues at hand. They meditate on the struggle, weigh out the options,
think about it some more, consider the outcomes both good and bad,
ponder even further, wonder how it could have been prevented in the
first place, and finally, exasperate themselves until their brain are utterly
and eventually exhausted. Before turning to anyone to talk about the
matter, they think about it to death.

Meet me.

This way of processing goes beyond my thought life and carries into
other areas of my life, like my passion for running. Since my early years
of college, I have been an on-again/off-again runner. I have run five
marathons, some more triumphantly than others. I have finished some
races strong. I've cheered on other runners and smiled for photo-ops to

create keepsakes that remain trophy treasures. But some races seem simply like a painful test of endurance. During those, I struggle to put one foot in front of the other and barely crawl across that finish line.

With each 26.2-mile race, I have committed myself to months of training runs. With each run, I have had countless hours of what I like to call "me time." In fact, one of the reasons I love pounding my feet against the pavement is that it gives me time to think. It's just me, God, and a few barking dogs. I have solved some of my biggest problems on a run (of course with the grace and understanding that comes through the Lord), whether it was a problem I was facing at work, a conflict in a relationship, or an issue that simply needed some thinking through. As an elementary school teacher, I planned some of my best teaching units during a thirty-minute run.

Internally, processing our problems can be a really healthy way to guide us towards a solution or success. It helps us to consider different perspectives, weigh out the options, consider the various outcomes, and lead us to a well-calculated decision.

But when processing turns into isolating ourselves and carrying the load all in our own strength, we may end up holding something that has the potential to be too great a weight for one person to bear. This type of heavy load is better shared with another person. It's like the old cartoon where the animated character held the anvil over his head, only to eventually be completely smooshed into the ground, leaving only the weight and his dusty remains. It's a comical example, and yet a very good depiction of what happens when we try to carry a burden that is entirely too large for us alone.

Raising children is a challenge. Can I say it again? Raising children is a challenge! And raising a child with special needs is an even greater challenge. We have burdens to bear and loads to carry each moment of each day—whether it's a meeting with a teacher who is concerned with our child's progress, or another medical bill that sits in the "to pay" pile while the bank account is sparse, or wondering if the prayer you just prayed for the millionth time will really be answered.

Don't Run Alone

It's a good thing I enjoy running because I married into a running family. They run, rain or shine, and they do it together. They do every training run together, whether it's a three-mile run or a twenty-mile run. They take the walk breaks together, bathroom stops together, they even share the same sports drink to hydrate together.

To me, the best run is the run I do alone. I love my family dearly, but when it comes to running, I love tuning out, listening to the sounds around me, and only worrying about the sound of my feet hitting the pavement. I want to take a drink break when I need one, stop and tie my shoe without holding up the whole group, and run at the pace that feels best for me. This carries into other parts of my life. I like my alone time. I am what you would consider an introvert; I become more energized when I am alone.

Though this is my approach with running and recharging, the support of community became important when I had Charlie. From the time the doctor first had concerns when I was twenty weeks pregnant, I knew self-sustainment wasn't an option. There is no way I could carry the weight of the decision making for her health. To yield the greatest results, I couldn't be the only one to do the follow-up therapy exercises at home. I couldn't be the only one going to the doctors' appointments and hearing the news, once again, that we need to keep an eye on things and come back in six months. I couldn't and I shouldn't. I praise the Lord and hope you do, too, that He designed us to need help, support, and community. Charlie has a mother *and* a father. She has faith-filled grandparents, compassionate aunts and uncles, and loving family friends. God knew what He was doing when He gave her to us—*all* of us.

Better Together

When we're talking about our relationship or life in general, my husband regularly repeats the phrase, "Better together." We know that the life we live together is better than what we would experience on our own. We have known each other for twelve years, been together for eleven, and married for eight. My life is better when Luke is part of it. He is my better half. The Lord gave me a God-fearing, brave, tender-hearted man who brings out the best in me and loves me even when I'm at my worst.

God knew what He was doing when He gave her to us—all of us.

We are committed to one another for life and we know that God has put us together as one to love each other, love our children, and advance His kingdom here on earth. I am better—a better person and especially a better parent—when Luke is by my side.

All parents carry the weight of raising their children. Whether or not our children have special needs, I believe we were meant to carry that weight together. We and our children will be better for it!

Every year, it seems as if Charlie's medical appointments fall around the same time. At first, I took her to each appointment since my husband works full time. I strapped my little Charlie girl in her car seat, and off we went to the cardiologist, the ophthalmologist, the audiologist, the radiologist, and the lab, all in addition to our regular well-child checkups, therapies, and Early-On school program.

Depending on the appointment, there could be tears from either or both of us. Let's just say I have mastered the art of restraining my daughter in various positions, for the least discomfort and maximum speed of getting the necessary exam completed. I have become quite the MMA (mixed martial arts) champion (in my own mind), wrestling my three year old just to keep her still long enough for the doctor to gather the data that helps us monitor her development.

I am sure you can relate. Your calendar is full each month, all in an attempt to raise your child and prepare him or her for the best future possible. You may be like I was at first, taking on the weight of all these appointments, not because your spouse or the other guardian had any ill intentions, but simply because you are the available parent.

Give Up

For the first several years, I bore the anxiety and stress of sitting through appointment after appointment with Charlie alone. And at most appointments, Charlie resisted the doctors' efforts and seemed more nervous than I was. Her fear increased my stress, and my stress increased her fears, and so on and so forth. So many times, I was the mother with tear-filled eyes, restraining my child yet again so the nurse could draw her blood, take an x-ray, or listen for her heart murmur. At each appointment, doctors shared critical results, shared any concerns, advised necessary follow-up testing, and occasionally gave the "everything looks great" update.

I didn't want to burden my husband by asking him to take time off work and come to appointments. There were times I even hesitated to tell him the doctor's report because I didn't want him to feel the weight, disappointment, and fear that I felt. I wanted to be Super-Mom and take care of it all myself. That was my first mistake.

But it wasn't long before I figured out that, if I went alone to all these weekly, monthly, and yearly visits, I would inevitably find myself overwhelmed, heavy hearted, and at my breaking point. I needed Luke. I needed to tell him that I needed him.

I remember coming to my husband one afternoon after taking Charlie to yet another specialist. We had visited the cardiologist that day. They performed an echo-cardiogram to monitor the holes that still remained in her heart. I was exhausted from wrestling with Charlie so the doctor could complete the test and from hearing once again that the results were inconclusive. I sat on the carpet in our family room, legs folded and looking up at Luke as he sat in our big, green chair. With Charlie down for her nap, this was our precious time alone.

"Honey, can I talk to you?" I started off strong, but soon my facade of strength disintegrated as I began to cry. "I can't do this by myself."

The word "can't" was a hard one to throw out there. I hated to even say the word. It made me feel like I wasn't strong enough, like I was a failure.

I still don't like admitting I can't do something. I want to be strong for my daughter. I want to be strong for my husband. I want to be strong for myself.

I know what you are probably thinking, and it's true—I was filled with pride. Part of being better together is admitting that you are not okay on your own. It's a humbling blow to your pride when you realize you can't do everything on your own. But for the sake of my mind, my heart, and my daughter, I needed to step up and give up. I had come to the end of my strength and I had a choice: I could either pretend I wasn't hurting and stumbling under the weight I carried, or I could choose to let someone help me. In that moment, I needed to admit to myself, to my husband, and to the Lord, that I wasn't strong enough. That's why Charlie has both of us—Momma and Dada. So we can be strong together.

I needed to step up and give up.

"I need you there with me."

My husband looked at me and responded immediately with words that brought the comfort and the support I needed. "I would love to be there." He wanted to be there for me, and all I had to do was ask.

Let the Better Begin

Maybe you are in a similar family situation and feel overwhelmed by the weight of caring for your child's well-being and future—the weekly schedule, the constant oversight, the task of ensuring your child is given every possible opportunity in spite of his or her disability. I am here to tell you from my heart to yours: You aren't alone! Stop trying to be the supermom (or dad). You may have a spouse who is ready to step in and carry the load with you. Invite him! Involve him! Include him! (I'm going to refer to your spouse as "him," for simplicity's sake, but please know that I recognize that you may be the primary caregiver and the husband.) Maybe your spouse wants to be more involved but just doesn't know how to yet. God's best for your child is both you and your spouse working together to raise and nurture him or her into God's destiny.

As couples, we have to function as one unit for the sake of our children. We need to stand together in prayer, in faith, in decision making, in the day-to-day care of the children we have been chosen to raise. We became one flesh with our spouses in God's eyes on the day we said, "I do." We must stand together in that one flesh as we parent! There is strength in numbers—both physically and spiritually!

Even if you don't have a spouse, you don't have to travel this road alone. I feel certain that you have other God-ordained, amazing, supportive individuals who are ready and waiting with open arms and helping hands. You may have a sibling, or parent, or friend who can and wants to be there for you. May I give you some advice? Don't wait till you find yourself broken on the carpet like I was. Let them help. Start the conversation. Start inviting others to join you on your journey. The more love, support, and care your child receives, the better!

Let others be there for you. Don't try to be strong on your own. You will only last so long until you hit a wall and the ugly-crying starts. You know what I'm talking about: that face you get when you cry and you want no one to see you. And the ugly-cry only gets uglier the longer you try to keep it together!

You may be tempted to give up, let stress overcome you, and walk in defeat and fear of the future. But we can hold onto the words in 1 Corinthians 10:13 that promises that "God is faithful, who will not allow you to be tempted beyond what you are able, but with the temptation will also make the way of escape, that you may be able to bear it." (NKJV).

God designed a plan that gives us a way out. And I believe that the way out is through those He has placed in our lives with whom we can link arms, share the load, and pray with through every season and challenge.

In Your Corner

In my experience, when I share this journey with several trusted, loving people in my life, I am better for it. I am a better mother, a better wife, and a better person in general when I open my life up to loved ones whom the Lord has purposefully placed in my corner.

I think of the boxer who has a coach in the corner of the boxing ring. The coach watches the fight unfold. He brings perspective and insight as he watches the opponent strike at the boxer's weak areas. The coach shouts encouragement when the boxer's head hangs low. Perhaps the fight gets harder and rougher than anyone ever imagined it would, but the coach stands in the corner offering support when the going gets tough. He cleans up the cuts and wounds that come with each round. Without that support, that strength waiting in the corner, the boxer most assuredly would be discouraged sooner, or worse, give up.

We are stronger when we enter a battle together—with one another and with God. And isn't this a battle that you and I are fighting for our children? We are fighting for them to develop and thrive as individuals and members of society.

How could one have chased a thousand, and two have put ten thousand to flight, unless their Rock had sold them, and the Lord had given them up?

—Deuteronomy 32:30 (ESV)

Luke and I are richly blessed to have a very involved family who will support, love, and go to the ends of the earth for Charlie. Since we talked, my husband goes to doctors' appointments and therapy sessions with me. My mother and mother-in-law have joined us in the classroom to meet Charlie's teachers and see all that Charlie is experiencing with other kids her age. My brother has rallied others, along with himself, to give generously to meet Charlie's medical needs. My family and friends have financially supported us and participated in a marathon to raise awareness and funds for a local support organization for families with children with Down syndrome. We have friends who faithfully pray for Charlie's health and development. God has surrounded Charlotte with people who want to be involved in her life—it isn't just me. I'm so thankful for that!

You aren't alone either. Look around you, to your spouse, extended family, friends, church family. Whether few or many, invite others into your life. Ask them for help on this journey of raising your child. Let them support you however they can. Chances are, they really do want to help—you only need to ask.

Power in Prayer

I find that as I lean on others—my husband, family members, and friends—I am strengthened. Knowing that I am not alone encourages me to keep pressing on. And even more than loved ones supporting us emotionally, physically, or financially, I have found a treasure in their spiritual support through prayer.

Whenever we are headed into a challenging situation with Charlie's health, I text our family and close friends and ask them to pray. I believe in the power of prayer. In James 5:16, it says that, "the prayer of a righteous person is powerful and effective" (NIV). I want as many powerful and effective prayers said for Charlie as possible! We know that God has a miraculous answer to every prayer.

It is so encouraging to know that we are not the only ones praying for her. We know that family and friends are interceding for her. They will better know how to pray as we share her needs, the breakthroughs we want as a family, and the test results.

Prayer is powerful! We need to pray for our children! We need other people to pray for our children! If they are going to pray, we have to open up and share with them how they can do so.

I encourage you to ask people in your life to pray for your child. Ask them to stand with you in faith for healing and breakthrough. Pray with them over the phone, ask them to pray while you are at the doctor, ask them to get others to pray as well!

There have been times when I didn't know how to pray for Charlie, but my mother did. There have been times when I have been discouraged or overwhelmed and in stubbornness of heart didn't pray, but my husband did. There have been times when I have been gripped by fear and felt as if I couldn't pray, but my sister did. I praise God for every person in Charlie's life who prays and believes great things for her life.

Remember, when we don't have the strength to pray, others do!

Together with God

In Charlie's first year, my emotions and mindset swung wildly from high to low. For a few months, I would be strong and positive. Nothing could discourage me when it came to Charlie's progress. In those times, I felt completely confident that God was working to build strength and peace in me that was beyond my understanding. I would find myself so happy just to be happy! I had the assumption that parents who raised children with special needs always carried a burden, a disappointment, or a sadness that things didn't turn out maybe how they expected (boy was I wrong—some of the most content and joy-filled people I know are raising children with special needs). So when I experienced genuine joy, I felt like God was really doing great work in me!

Then out of nowhere, the tiniest situation would arise. Someone would make a comment about Charlie at the grocery store or my mind would begin to wonder and worry about the future—*Will Charlie ever get married? Will she go to college? What if someone ever tried to take advantage of her?* I would soon find myself lying in my bed crying, not knowing why God chose me to be Charlie's mother because I didn't feel smart enough, strong enough, or simply able enough to be what she needed me to be. My heart sank to such a deep, dark, empty, hopeless place that it made me wonder if I would even be able to keep going. After being in such a place of confidence and joy, I felt guilty for falling to such a low, as if by doing so, I was denying the work of God in my life. On those days, I felt like I was back to square one.

Maybe you have also felt the emotional pendulum swings while raising your child. There are moments, days, and months of victory and joy where you feel as though you have overcome all doubt and fear and are walking in strength with a faith-filled perspective. Then, for no significant reason, you suddenly find yourself broken and defeated. It may have been caused by another day of what feels like no progress. Or perhaps you just had too much time to yourself and began to fear the near or distant future.

I believe we all have these ups and downs. In the valleys and on the mountain tops, be assured that as Christians, we have the answer. We can take comfort in knowing that, when we "pass through the waters, [God] will be with [us]; and through the rivers, they shall not overwhelm [us]; when [we] walk through the fire [we] shall not be burned, and the flame shall not consume [us]" (Isaiah 43:2, ESV).

In my despair, when Charlie was several months old, I lay on my bed, staring at the wall, wondering if I could or should let the tears flow yet again. I could either bottle it up, press it down (and wait for a later, bigger explosion), or be honest in the moment and cry out to God. So I asked God, "Is this okay? Can I be here again?"

I didn't know if I *could* come to God any time I was in tears and overwhelmed. Would God be sick of me crying about this? Would He be mad that I had taken that comment from the grocery store clerk so personally? I wasn't sure if I needed to pull myself together and tough it out each time I faced bumps in the road—whether it was a small speed bump or another mountain that needed to be moved. When I asked Him in my spirit, I heard the Lord say,

As long as you bring it to me…

I let this phrase sink into my heart. *As long as I bring it to Him, this is okay, because I am in the right place, at the feet of the Father.*

At His Feet

I use the phrase "at His feet" because it reminds me of the woman who comes to the feet of Jesus in Luke 7. She comes to Him broken, raw, and hurting. Though the disciples are disgusted by her sin and reputation of being a wayward woman, Jesus is moved with compassion and doesn't drive her away. It's at His feet that her healing begins. It's at His feet that her pain is healed by His love. It's at the feet of Jesus where we, as parents, can find God's love and comfort in our distress. It's here that we can be renewed when we are weary.

As long as I bring it to Him, this is okay, because I am in the right place, at the feet of the Father.

If we go through a dark day, week, month, or year and try to tough it out on our own with small pep talks and looking within to muster up the strength, then there would be a problem—a big problem. But if we take it to God each time, whether the matter is huge or small, we can know that we are in the best position possible. We can have rough days and be honest about it as long as we bring it to the Lord. When we are in a posture of prayer and humility before the Lord, He enables us to find greater strength and ultimate victory as His power flows through our lives. It's best to bring our hurt, unmet expectations, fears, and pain to God because He is our supply, our anchor, our rock to stand on!

Lighten Up

But he said to me, 'My grace is sufficient for you, for my power is made perfect in weakness.' Therefore I will boast all the more gladly about my weaknesses, so that Christ's power may rest on me.
—2 Corinthians 12:9 (NIV)

Let God in on your weaknesses. Let Him into the dark places so that He can bring in His light. Let Him make you strong and help you overcome. In this calling of parenthood, we were never meant to do it alone or in our own strength. We will come to the end of our strength and resources—the end of ourselves—time and time again. And honestly, our kids need God working through us so that they can live out their fullest potential and purpose in Him.

For Charlie's sake, I have to turn to God in my weakness. I have to let God in to my situation and let Him help me. Likewise, your child needs you to experience God's help—His grace and power.

Every time we feel weighed down, can't sleep, can't think straight because of the concerns we have about our kids' well-being, we are doing something wrong. But doing the right thing is simple. Matthew 11:30 tells us that God's "yoke is easy and {His} burden is light" (NIV). When we are walking with the Lord and trusting in Him, then the heavy burdens are gone. They are His because we cast our cares upon Him (1 Peter 5:7).

Are you casting your cares on Him? Are you throwing the weight of your worries onto His broad shoulders? Or are you carrying them? It's time to "lighten up" your load because He cares for you. We serve a good and loving God who doesn't want us to do this alone. He has placed people in our lives to lean on, and He Himself designed it so that He can come in, and bring strength and peace to every situation. As He does this, it shows how kind, generous, loving, and powerful He is. Through these situations, He glorifies Himself.

Start Now

I encourage you, if you haven't already, to ask others—your spouse, your family, your friends—to join you in your journey, to help you, and pray with you. If you don't have people in your life at this very moment that you can imagine bringing into your corner, then you can ask God to bring them! James 4:2 says, "You do not have because you do not ask God" (NIV). So start asking God to put these people into your life! (Go ahead, ask Him right now. I'll wait.)

I found encouragement and support outside of family and friends in an organization I discovered online. I was amazed at how many local organizations showed up in my search engine when I typed in "support for parents of kids with Down syndrome." I made some phone calls, submitted my email address, and before I knew it, additional support arrived! I got phone calls from mentor parents, invitations to meetings and "Moms' Night Out" events, and newsletters with support that I so desperately needed. Pull others close and you will be better for it!

When you share the journey with others, you can wait, and trust God together, and celebrate together. This will give your child a stronger support system that will lead them to live a more loving and secure life. And as you let your spouse in, your family in and friends in, the most important thing is to let the Lord in. He is the only One who can satisfy what your heart really needs.

In the next chapter, we will talk about the best thing you can do for your child as you stand together with others! It is the key to miracles, healing, and a breakthrough for your child!

6
Power of Prayer

The effectual fervent prayer of a righteous man availeth much.
—James 5:16 (KJV)

I believe that I am who I am today because of something my mother has done since before I was born. Something she has dedicated herself to faithfully, selflessly, and passionately. Something she did in what scripture calls "the secret place," with other believers, and with also me as she tucked me into bed each night. My mother has been, and continues to be, a woman of prayer.

For more than twenty years now, she has gathered with other Christian mothers who choose to stand in faith for their children through prayer. She has "prayed the scriptures" over my life and interceded for me in every season of life as a young child, an ornery teenager, a busy college student, a working woman, a new wife, and now a mother.

"Praying the scriptures" is simply asking God to do what His Word promises He will do. Entire books have been written about it by Bible scholars as well as those who have simply discovered how wonderful and effective it is.

In Psalm 103:20 it says:

Bless the LORD, you angels who belong to him, you mighty warriors who carry out his commands, who are obedient to the sound of his words. (NIV)

So my mother made a habit of finding those scripture verses (His Words) and praying them for those she loved.

I believe her prayers helped me to hear the call of God for my life, find and marry a man who loves God and loves me, and to know the will of God and experience His provision, peace, and protection on a daily basis. My mother's prayers are precious and priceless to me. Her faithful example taught me what a mother can be for her children—a prayer warrior momma.

A Mother's Son

There is a mother in scripture who challenges me to be relentless and passionate in my pursuit of God Almighty through prayer for my children. It's the compelling story of a Shunammite woman in 2 Kings 4, which begins with the prophet Elisha passing through her town. She urges him to stay for a meal and he agrees. While enjoying her continued hospitality, Elisha prophesies that she will be blessed with a son despite her previous barrenness and her husband's advanced age.

Better than any thank you card or flowers, she is given a child to love, nurture, and raise. She must have loved having a little tyke running around her house. I imagine him, just as any boy, loving the outdoors, wrestling with his daddy, and making messes—yet being so easy to forgive when all he did was look in his mother's eyes. Boys have a way of melting their mommas' hearts.

But this sweet story quickly takes a frightening turn:

The child grew, and one day he went out to his father, who was with the reapers. He said to his father, "My head! My head!" His father told a servant, "Carry him to his mother." After the servant had lifted him up and carried him to his mother, the boy sat on her lap until noon, and then he died.

—2 Kings 4:18-20 (NIV)

One moment the boy was in the fields alongside his father, the next, he was breathing his last breath with his mother. Reading this, I imagine what I might feel and do if I were in this woman's shoes. I would be heartbroken, hysterical. I doubt that I would have the presence of mind to do what she did next.

After watching her son die, she rushes him to the bedroom that had been constructed for the prophet who had given her the promise of her now-dead son. She lays him on the bed, shuts the door, and sets out to find Elisha. In the verses to follow, I see two things that set her apart as a mother; two things that call me to a higher level.

Keep Focus

First of all, her response is not one of panic or heartache, but strategy and intentionality that leads her to the man of God. Elisha is her connection to the Living God and she knows that He is the answer for her son. She doesn't call her girlfriends to cry and mourn about the situation. In fact, she didn't even explain to her husband what was going on. She had no time to lose. She sets out to find Elisha at Mount Carmel.

Can you relate to the situation this mother faced? She had a hopeless and dire report. But look at how she responds to this tragedy. Without missing a step, she gets right down to business by going to God. I want my response to be like this if Charlotte gets a negative report from the doctor or when we need God to intervene and perform the miraculous. How easy it is to call my mother, my sister, my husband when I get a report from the doctor that Charlotte's echo-cardiogram is inconclusive, or hear from her therapists that they aren't seeing the progress they'd hoped for, or get a call from a nurse who wants us to come in for more blood work (yet again) to rule out any disease or illness. Though others may bring encouragement or offer a prayer that sets our hearts at ease, we know the strong Tower, the Rock to stand on, the Healer who can bring the answer we need for our children (Proverbs 18:10, Psalm 18:2, 1 Peter 2:24).

Let me challenge you to cut out the middle man (mother, sister, friend, or husband) when you receive challenging news! Take your concerns directly to our Heavenly Father; pray before reaching out to family or friends when you are in a moment of pain over your child. I have spent many car rides home from the doctor's office crying out to God, knowing that, before I even think about reaching out to anyone, I better reach out to God. Because everything Charlotte needs, everything I need is found in the miracle-working power of God. I hold onto the verse of scripture in Philippians 4:19 that promises that God shall meet all my needs according to His riches and glory.

Before I even think about reaching out to anyone, I better reach out to God.

Not only does this mother keep her focus on the Lord in her time of need, but I also see a mother who isn't quick to let worry arise. So often as parents, we assume the worst; we imagine the tragedy that might await. Rather than acting in fear and letting an anxious spirit well up, I try to always remember to set my focus, my mind, on the One who has the answer. Rather than give into the temptation of fear and worry, I try to see that temptation as a challenge to obey the scriptures and take every thought captive to make it obedient and honoring to Christ (2 Corinthians 10:5).

Relentless Prayer

The second thing I love about this mother is what she does when she gets to the prophet. So often our prayers can be casual or even distracted amidst keeping a clean and orderly home. I am guilty of losing focus during my prayer time all because out of the corner of my eye, I notice how badly I need to dust my mantle, or see the notification that just popped up on my phone, or am reminded that I need to walk the dog as I watch my neighbors responsibly and lovingly walking theirs. To the contrary, this mother is on a mission and nothing and no one will stop her!

Elisha sees this focused and passionate mother coming towards him. Hoping to quickly address her need, he sends his servant to meet her. But when approached by his servant, she passes right by him and determinedly continues towards Elisha. When she finally gets to him, she takes hold of his feet and cries out so that her son can be healed.

I love the posture this mother has at the feet of the man of God. She has no shame, all pride is pushed aside as she begs for her son's life. What a picture for us to model our prayer lives after. Get down and dirty and intercede for our child's miracle.

This communicates something to us about praying for our children in times of need. We can come raw and desperate before God with our petitions. There is no formality or legality at the feet of Jesus. I do believe that we ought to honor the Lord and be reverent in His presence, but to be real and transparent in our time of need is permitted and powerful.

Get down and dirty and intercede for our child's miracle.

Not only did the Shunammite mother throw herself at the feet of Elisha and beg for her son's healing, but she also refused to leave with his servant to do the healing. She wanted Elisha to travel back home with her and heal her son. She wouldn't settle for anything less. This challenges me to faithfully find the answer at the feet of Jesus and no one else—no doctor, therapist, or specialist. They may be the earthly tools of God's hand for healing, but God Himself is the ultimate healer (Psalm 107:19-20).

In Luke 18, there is a story of a widow who appears before a judge who did not fear the Lord or care about the approval of men. The widow comes to the ungodly judge over and over, pleading for justice against her enemy. After much persistence, he tires of her pleas and grants her request. We should be stirred by the verse that follows;

> *"And will not God bring about justice for his chosen ones, who cry out to him day and night? Will he keep putting them off? I tell you, he will see that they get justice and quickly…"*
>
> *—Luke 18:7-8 (NIV)*

God *hears* the relentless prayer. God *responds* to the relentless prayer. He is our good judge who will hear our petitions for our children.

How to Pray

God wants to hear from us, but when we first received Charlie's diagnosis, I could barely talk to God about everything racing through my mind. I knew I needed to pray, but I didn't know how. *Do I pray for healing? How do I pray for something I know nothing about? What will her life be like? Since the spectrum for Down syndrome is so wide, how do I know what she will struggle with?*

In this state of being utterly overwhelmed, I looked to what I did know. I looked to what I could count on—the Word of God. The Scriptures offer truth for every situation; when read in context, the Bible demonstrates the goodness, faithfulness, and deep love of God. The Word gave me something to hold onto each day to give me strength, peace, and perspective. I sat in Charlie's room and read through a chapter of Psalms each day.

As I read, I wrote down scriptures that moved me or spoke to my heart. Those scriptures then guided my prayers for Charlie. I wrote down and posted each verse up on a prayer board and stared at those words each time I went into her bedroom. I still treasure the truths God gave me to hold onto and believe for myself and my family.

I've include just a few of those verses and the prayers that came from them below. I hope these words will encourage your heart. If you are not sure how to pray for your child and family, please feel free to use these verses and prayers as a starting point.

"The Lord will perfect that which concerns me; Your mercy, O Lord, endures forever; Do not forsake the works of Your hands."
—Psalm 138:8 (NKJV)

Lord, please perfect everything that concerns me about Charlie. Perfect her health and well-being. Thank You for Your mercy each day. I believe You will not forsake our family or our daughter because we are the work of Your hands.

"I lie down and sleep; I wake again because the Lord sustains me."
—Psalm 3:5 (NIV)

Thank You, Lord, that You sustain me. That You will help me to sleep at night and wake up in the morning and keep going.

"Know that the Lord has set apart the godly for himself; the Lord will hear when I call to him."
— Psalm 4:3 (NIV)

Thank You, Lord, that I am set apart for You. I am not set apart for destruction or darkness, but for You, God. Thank You that You hear me even now, as I call out to You.

"... the Lord has heard my weeping."
— Psalm 6:8 (NIV)

Thank You, Lord, that my tears are noticed by You. Thank You that You see me and are with me in my sadness.

I went through the Psalms, verse by verse, and wrote down each meaningful and ministering scripture. As I posted them and prayed over these scriptures each day, my soul was strengthened and encouraged by the Word of God.

When I didn't have my own words, I prayed God's Word—just as my mother had taught me was most effective. And each day as I prayed, I got a little stronger. I found hope, peace, and grace through prayer. There is a reason we are commanded to pray without ceasing in 1 Thessalonians 5:17. Because prayer works! Prayer is powerful! Prayer does more than change situations: it gives God our permission for Him to change us!

Just a few short months after Charlie was born, I joined my husband for his staff retreat with fellow church pastors and leaders. This was a time of connecting and refreshing for the pastoral staff and their spouses. We were having a night of worship and prayer together when the children's pastor walked over to me and handed me a small, white piece of paper. On it was written:

"That person is like a tree planted by streams of water, which yields its fruit in season and whose leaf does not wither—whatever they do prospers."
—Psalm 1:3 (NIV)

She told me to hold onto this verse for my daughter. And I have! The words are written on a blue sticky note and posted in my prayer closet (I'll share more about that later) to guide my prayers. I pray with faith every day that Charlie will be a like a tree—flourishing and producing fruit in every season, not withering but prospering spiritually, mentally, emotionally, physically, and relationally.

I look realistically at what is going on in the natural (earthly) realm, and I intercede for my daughter in the spiritual realm with my prayers, asking God to intervene and do wonderful things in her and through her. Some people call this intercession, or interceding in prayer, on another's behalf.

Big Prayers

As Christians, we believe God is our Healer who works miracles. He gives the blind their sight, makes the lame walk, opens the ears of the deaf, heals the leper, raises the dead (Mark 8:25, John 5:8, Mark 7:35, Luke 17:14, John 11:43-44). There is no limit to His power! I have grown up reading about miraculous healings in the Scriptures, heard others' testimonies of radical encounters with God that healed them, and even seen healings take place in church services, prayer meetings, and various other God-appointed healing moments.

In all honesty, I didn't know how to feel about praying for Charlie's ultimate healing. Because in a way, I felt like if I prayed for her to be something that she is not, I wasn't fully accepting her as she was. If I pray for healing, am I rejecting the way God made her? I want to love her just as she is and not spend my life wishing and praying she be something else.

This is something I still battle with from time to time, but I have somewhat of a resolution. Do I love Charlotte just as she is? Absolutely! But do I want my child to have health issues of any kind? No. I don't want Charlie to ever have a surgery, or struggle with a disease, or miss out on life due to her diagnosis. So I am not praying that God changes the beautiful, sweet, precious gift that He has given us, but I am believing and asking for God to do the impossible, prove doctors wrong, break the mold and expectations of what my Charlie will experience in this life. I want my daughter to thrive physically, mentally, emotionally, and socially. And that is a good prayer to pray!

Commit to the Process

So many times I have prayed and prayed for some specific breakthrough for Charlotte. I fast, I intercede, praying with all the boldness and faith I can muster. There are nights I have stood over her crib, quietly crying and interceding for weaknesses to become strengths and limitations to disappear.

There are some instances when God has answered my prayers and performed a miracle in a moment. We rejoice and celebrate these victories and give God glory for answering our request. Then there are other times when the limitation or weakness remains, and I have to choose to continue to pray and hope. Some prayers are answered instantly, while others are uttered year after year. All the while, God is teaching me to commit to the process.

In 2 Kings 5, a man named Naaman, a mighty soldier and army commander, contracted the devastating disease, leprosy. He was a respected man, and it's quite possible he had a promising future—until the leprosy threatened his way of life. When he sought healing from the prophet Elisha, he was told to go wash himself seven times in the Jordan River. It wasn't a one-time washing that would heal him, but a process of seven washings. It was only after experiencing the process that Naaman would see the miracle of his healing.

Though reluctant at first (the Jordan did not provide ideal washing waters for a man of dignity), Naaman submitted to the process and was washed clean of leprosy!

Sometimes God heals in a moment, but other times, a process and testing comes before the healing. The Lord may ask us to pray the same prayer of healing for our children for months, years, even decades. Are we willing to commit to the process? I want to pray right on through to the miracle. What if Naaman had only washed himself six times? He would have been just one step away from being healed of leprosy. May God give us grace to finish the race set before us (Hebrews 12:1-2) and not grow weary as we pray for our children.

Make Room

I have to share with you something special that has recently developed in my house, up in my bedroom, and amidst my dirty clothes hamper. I am now the proud owner of a prayer closet! Perhaps you have heard of this special place before. A prayer closet is an area where you can get some alone time to pray. This is a place of privacy and seclusion that can ensure time spent with God will be uninterrupted and productive. For years, I had heard of other believers having these prayer closets, but the thought of sitting in a cold, messy closet baffled me. I thought I would be too distracted by the half-hung clothes and disorderly shoes scattered across the carpet floor.

After years of wondering, I decided it was time to put the wonderings to rest. I thought maybe this could be a good thing for me since prayer was an area of my life God was challenging me to grow in. So one day, I cleared the floor, pushed back the hampers, and posted up some scriptures that I wanted to pray for my husband, myself, and my children. Then I closed the door, got down on my knees, and to my amazement … it was silent … and perfect. My new prayer closet was just the setting I needed to tune out distraction, be quiet before God, and intercede in a greater way than I ever had before.

I don't share this with you to sell the idea of prayer closets. What I hope to convince you of is the importance of making room (pardon the pun) for prayer in our lives. When we do, God will show us how to pray for our children and that greater breakthrough is ahead. So I encourage you to boldly pray, relentlessly pray, commit to the process, and trust God with your child.

I want to exhaust myself in prayer for my children.

I want to be a mother who prays, who sees the wonderful things God does because I asked Him to move forward with the wonderful plans He has for my children. When Charlotte is grown, I want to look back at the years of raising her and know that I prayed relentlessly and passionately. I don't want to wish I prayed more boldly or fasted more faithfully; I want to see her life woven together and miracles accomplished as a result of the mighty hand of God working in her life in response to prayer. I would hate to wonder what her life could have been if I sought the Lord more on her behalf. I want to exhaust myself in prayer for my children. I want carpet burns on my knees from interceding and crying out to God. I want to run out of tears because I have pleaded and given everything at His feet. I want to be a prayer warrior for my family, just like my mother was a prayer warrior for me.

Prayer is a powerful tool for parents. I also believe that our child's progress and breakthrough comes not only through prayer but that we need to get a little dirty and start digging to see the miracles we so desperately pray for!

7
Dig Ditches

In the same way, faith by itself, if it is not accompanied by action, is dead.
—James 2:17 (NIV)

When I was ten, a friend invited me to go with her family to the mountains for the weekend. Our time would be spent four wheeling, hiking, and venturing through the wilderness. I was so excited. I couldn't wait to go somewhere I had never been and do something I had never done.

We spent our nights in the family camper and our days out on the mountain side. One afternoon, we begged my friend's mom to let us take the four wheelers out by ourselves to ride the trails and find adventure. Her mother was hesitant because the gray sky suggested rain. The last thing she wanted was for us to get far away from the family camper in the pouring rain and possibly get the four wheelers stuck in the mud. She spoke from experience—a mother's wisdom, of course.

After much pleading, she reluctantly allowed us to go out for a short time, but she warned, "If it starts to rain, you must come back!" We eagerly promised and hit the trails!

It wasn't long into our adventure when a lone drop of water fell from a sky, then another and another. Before we knew it, what began as a few drops turned into a downpour. We didn't want to turn back, but with each pull of the throttle, we were reminded of my friend's mother instructing us to, "Come back!" To avoid punishment—and the downer that would be set on the weekend—we headed back.

As we raced back to the camper, we came upon a ravine. When we had crossed it before, this same spot was a dry ditch that we barely noticed crossing. But now, with buckets of water falling from the sky, it was a muddy mess that would be difficult to pass through. I remember staring at the ravine with my friend, wondering if we should go for it— and with the wisdom one has at the ripe old age of ten, we did just that! We revved up the gas and plowed not *through* but right *into* the ravine. We were stuck. Terribly stuck.

Have you ever been stuck? Maybe you have been stuck in a relationship or in a conflict at work. Or maybe there is a family matter you just can't get through. Maybe you feel yourself stuck financially or physically—unable to improve your circumstances.

Let's apply this concept to our children. Do you ever feel stuck with your child's progress, like you are in a valley, where you so desperately need a miracle to happen? Me too.

Unexpected Challenge

Scripture tells of three kings gathered together to travel through the Desert of Edom to fight Moab. Due to rebellion and unmet expectations, the king of Israel, along with the king of Judah and the king of Edom, were on a mission. They set out to bring justice but were met with a problem along the way. We see something epic unfold in 2 Kings 3:9-10 (NIV):

> *So the king of Israel set out with the king of Judah and the king of Edom. After a roundabout march of seven days, the army had no more water for themselves or for the animals with them. "What!" exclaimed the king of Israel. "Has the Lord called us three kings together only to hand us over to Moab?"*

The kings ran into an unexpected challenge. I am sure when they set out on their mission they never intended to run out of water, for if they knew, they would have prepared better to ensure their water supply would be more than enough for them, their men, and their animals.

This reminds me of the art of leaving home with our children. In order to guarantee a successful mission, be it a trip to the park on a sunny day or a run to the grocery store, we must prepare for the mission at hand.

Sippy cup? *Check.*

Cheerios? *Check.*

Extra diapers? *Check.*

Wipes? *Check.*

Change of clothes? *Check.*

Hat? *Check.*

Sunglasses? *Check.*

Phone? *Check.*

Wallet? *Check.*

Keys? *Check.*

Happy child (at the moment)? *Check!*

We do everything we can to ensure we're equipped for a win. And sometimes, we do win. We remember every teeny, tiny item. We have the snacks and sippy cup in hand ready to pass off at the perfect moment.

We do everything we can to ensure we're equipped for a win. And sometimes, we do win.

We avoid disaster by doing diaper changes and potty runs at the just the right time. We keep the car ride fun with sing-alongs and silly faces—and we enjoy the "perfect" outing.

But sometimes, even when we have every good intention and leave armed and ready, we find ourselves, much like these kings, yelling out, "What? This was supposed to be an easy outing!"

Move Toward Your Miracle

These kings were at a standstill. They needed a miracle and fast! One of the king's officers recalls Elisha, the prophet. Though Elisha resists at first, he agrees to help the kings and seeks God on their behalf.

> *While the harpist was playing, the hand of the Lord came upon Elisha and he said, "This is what the Lord says: Make this valley full of ditches. For this is what the Lord says: You will see neither wind nor rain, yet this valley will be filled with water, and you, your cattle, and your other animals will drink. This is an easy thing in the eyes of the Lord; he will also hand Moab over to you."*
>
> *—2 Kings 3: 15-18 (NIV)*

A miracle was around the corner for this army, but it didn't come without effort on their parts. They needed to start digging. God was going to rescue them, come to their aid, but they needed to take the first action step and dig the very ditches that God would fill with water.

Imagine the student who wants to get a good grade in his chemistry class. He needs this final class to graduate, so he prays to the Lord to help him pass the class. He would be a fool to think that all he needed to do was pray to get a passing grade to move on to graduation. No! He needs to pay attention in class, do his assignments, study for his tests, and complete his projects to the best of his ability. He needs to dig, and with the Lord's help, he will have the great testimony at the end that he passed.

Or let's say you want to have a long, healthy life, free from health issues or major setbacks that hinder you or limit your days here on earth.

Well, you would be quite silly to share that petition with the Lord, then each night sit on your couch eating chocolate cookies and ice cream, burgers and soda five times a week, and never break a sweat at the gym. No, you would do your part. You would do your best to eat right, exercise, and be consistent with your checkups with the doctor. You need to break a sweat because you're digging, digging, digging.

Desperation Leads to Digging

These three kings were in a place of desperation. They needed God to intervene. How many times have you been there? Maybe not on the literal battlefield, but the battlefield for your child, desperate for God to intervene and bring break through. I have found myself in this position countless times.

I so desperately want God to heal Charlie's heart. I pray that the doctor's report shows a healthy, whole heart that functions properly in every way.

I so desperately want for Charlie to have a breakthrough with her speech. I want her tongue to be able to form sounds and syllables, to open the way for clear communication.

I so desperately want her blood tests to come back showing nothing but a healthy little girl.

I so desperately want Charlie's mind to develop and for her to exceed any expectation or norm set for her by teachers or doctors.

I so desperately want to see Charlie be fully accepted by her peers so that she never is bullied or suffers from rejection or cruelty from others.

In this desperation, my best offense is first to seek the face of God. As I mentioned earlier, there is power in prayer. Elisha sought God on behalf of the kings, and in God's mercy and grace, He spoke. I see the example that I am first and foremost to pray about all things. And as I pray, I believe I am called to action—I must dig!

Grab a Shovel

I spent many hours in the backyard with my older siblings, shovels in hand. Although we spent most of our energy at odds with one another, this was one event that rallied us as one to accomplish a great feat—to dig the deepest hole possible. With dirt under our nails, we kneeled on the ground taking turns jumping into the hole. I remember the excitement when we would reach different depths which we measured with our bodies—knee deep, waist deep, chest deep, head deep, and even deeper! And boy, did it take work! We could work our hands to blisters. But it was always such a sense of accomplishment to step back and see the hole, that deep, deep hole. We knew we had successfully completed our task. Funny how simple the entertainment can be as a child; once finishing the hole, we celebrated our success, filled it up (per mom's request), only to return to dig once again.

As we so desperately want to see healing for our child—a breakthrough mentally, emotionally, physically—we need to first pray and then grab a shovel! These men who desperately needed water didn't just sit back and wait for God to do all the work; they took the first step and dug ditches. I am sure they got dirty, got blisters, and got tired.

When we seek God for our children, we don't just sit back and wait for Him to come and fix everything. Now, let me say that we serve a God who is totally able. Nothing is impossible for Him (Luke 1:37). He doesn't *need* our efforts. Rather, I believe He invites us to put our faith into action and be a part of the miracle that can happen for our child.

So as I desperately cry out to God for Charlie's speech to develop, I will dig ditches. I will research speech therapists. I will take her to therapy. I will be faithful to do the assigned exercises to help her with letter identification and enunciation.

And as I ask God to strengthen her muscles and ligaments, I will dig ditches. I will put on her braces each day and follow through with the orthopedist's advice to help her develop.

Now you may think I sound silly, stating the obvious. Of course, you will help your child and do anything and everything to help them thrive. Maybe you are a super parent who doesn't have days like I do—days when I just want Charlie to be a toddler. Days when I don't want her to get poked with a needle so doctors can do more blood work. Days when I don't want to spend our family time at home making her do exercises when she would rather play by her own rules. Days when I don't want to go to therapists' and doctors' appointments. Days when I want her to be a kid and stay in her pajamas until noon if she wants. Days when I just want my daughter to have an easy day. Days when I want an easy day.

But 2 Kings 3 challenges me. As I seek God for miracles for my Charlie, I have to grab a shovel and do my part. And as I do, His miracle is on the other side of my obedience!

Gold Digger

Let's talk about finances. I think this is one of the biggest challenges we face as parents raising children with special needs. The finances required to help our children succeed can lead to stress, sleepless nights, and constant budget adjustments. This has been one of the biggest areas where we have had to dig ditches. Yet it has also been the area in which we have seen God do the miraculous! We have had many different "dig sites" in obtaining the funds required for hospitable bills, medical equipment, and therapies.

The first time I started digging was not for our benefit but for the benefit of a local family support group which had been a big part of our story when Charlie was first born. This group provided a mentor mother for me, educational materials, monthly emails and newsletters, and provided the emotional and relational support we needed in our new season of parenting. I wanted to give back to those who had given us so much! I started by looking at what was in my hand.

Here's what I mean: When Moses stood before God, he was asked, "What is that in your hand?" (Exodus 4:2, NIV). Moses wasn't sure how he would deliver the Israelites and lead them to the Promised Land, but God assured him that all Moses needed was already in his hand—his staff. It was that same staff that turned water into blood and became a serpent before Pharaoh, thus, eventually causing Pharaoh to let God's people go, demonstrating the power of the one true God (Exodus 7:10, 20). So what was in my hand? What was a part of my life that I could use to help raise funds for this organization? My passion for running.

I signed up to run a marathon. By sending out letters to request support, blasting social media, and selling T-shirts, we were able to raise a significant amount of money for the organization. I was amazed at how many people wanted to show their support and love for Charlie and kids just like her. When I used what was in my hand to gather the funds, they came flooding in. God filled a ditch!

Another way we dug a ditch for a financial miracle was similar to how missionaries raise support for their work. Through the help of a user-friendly website, I created a profile page and a letter communicating Charlie's current medical needs and simply asked friends and family to consider being a part of Charlie's journey to continue to thrive and reach her full potential. God provided miraculously through others by taking care of the costs of surgeries and braces. We are regularly amazed at how God filled our ditches!

What is in your hand? Is it something you could use to dig a ditch for the financial miracle needed for your child's breakthrough?

I have spent hours researching what our state does for families raising children with disabilities. I have applied for grants and filled out applications for financial assistance. We have adjusted our family budget time and time again. We have said no to vacations and activities we wanted because we knew that we needed to dig a ditch. As we continue to seek God and trust Him to provide, we will be faithful to do our part and dig ditches for Charlie.

Don't Despise the Method

Now let me share with you something that God had to teach me. It's something I am not very proud of. At our church, we have an opportunity to go forward for prayer during the worship portion of our service. Almost every Sunday, people walk forward in faith and ask God to meet a need in their lives. Many times, my husband and I have gone forward for our Charlie—whether it's a prayer for physical or financial help—we continue to need God to intervene.

It became known to several other church members that we had a financial need for Charlie. Moved by our need and filled with compassion, a generous individual wanted to give our family a gift of money. I wanted God to provide, but for some reason the way He wanted to fill this ditch was difficult for me to accept. Maybe it was my pride, but something in me didn't want the miracle to come in that way. It is a humbling thing to have someone hand you a check when you don't have a way to repay them or thank them in a way that feels adequate.

Earlier I mentioned Naaman, the army commander who had leprosy. Naaman heard of the great man of God, Elisha, who could possibly bring healing and rid him of his skin disease. So he set out with hope and arrived at the door of Elisha's house. Elisha didn't answer the door and didn't even come out to speak to Naaman. Instead, he sent a messenger out to him, saying:

> *"Go, wash yourself seven times in the Jordan, and your flesh will be restored and you will be cleansed." But Naaman went away angry and said, "I thought that he would surely come out to me and stand and call on the name of the Lord his God, wave his hand over the spot and cure me of my leprosy. Are not Abana and Pharpar, the rivers of Damascus, better than all the waters of Israel? Couldn't I wash in them and be cleansed?"*

> —2 Kings 5:10-12 (NIV)

Naaman wanted God to heal him, but he was particular about how he wanted God to do it. He despised the idea of getting into the Jordan River. If God was going to perform a miracle for him, he preferred it to come in some other way.

I felt the same about the person who wanted to give us the money to help with Charlie's medical expenses. Although I had prayed for God to provide, I didn't feel comfortable accepting the provision in this way. I was just as stubborn as Naaman. My pride was blocking the blessing.

Naaman swallowed his pride, dipped in the Jordan seven times, and was healed (2 Kings 5:14). Although it was not the method he imagined, he submitted to God's plan and experienced God's healing power.

God corrected me in my pride as well. After telling Luke that I felt we should return the gift to this generous individual (trying to disguise my pride), he said that this person was determined to give and we ought to accept it. And in bringing my wrestling thoughts to the Lord, I felt

God invites us to be a part of the miracles that await our children.

Him soften my heart to receive His provision, even if it came in a way I didn't expect. We gratefully accepted the monetary gift He had provided. We were able to pay for Charlotte's medical bills and rejoiced over God's faithfulness to fill our valley with water from heaven.

Accept Your Invitation

God invites us to be a part of the miracles that await our children. Though He doesn't need us, He allows us to participate in the provision—whether it's providing healing, finances, or any type of break-through. I challenge you to not just sit back, but to accept your invitation to risk a few blisters and get a little sweaty along the way!

So let's be parents who pray *and* dig! Let's do our part to receive the miracles God has waiting for us in the valley. Grab a shovel and don't be afraid of getting dirty. God will honor our efforts, continue to order our steps, and lead our children into the fullness of His will!

8
God Encounters

*In the same way, let your light shine before others, that they may see your good
deeds and glorify your father in heaven.*
—Matthew 5:16 (NIV)

Have you ever had the luxury of walking up to a building where
someone stands ready to open the door? Your greeter may even be wear-
ing a fancy suit or nice black hat, all dressed and prepared to receive you
as a guest into whatever establishment you are entering.

As a mother with young children, I often have a full load in my arms
as I travel about. I have learned the art of resting a car seat on one hip,
hoisting a diaper bag over my shoulder, positioning a pink ladybug back-
pack perfectly on my other arm, and reserving the other hand for a tiny,
sweaty palm placed gently, but firmly (so as to not let her tiny feet make
a break for it) in mine.

I like to refer to this as the "lock and load" method. Often when
people offer to take something off my hands and help me to where I am
going, I am hesitant to say yes due to the perfect balance I have achieved.
I fear that if they take just one item, I might fall over entirely, and the
"lock and load" will turn into the "crash and burn."

With arms full, I know my Sunday mornings will be a little bit easier
as I head from my car to the front door of my church. Many times on my

way into the building, a smiling greeter awaits to hold the door open for me and my family, so we can come into the sanctuary and experience a precious time of worship—a God encounter. Yes, I could open the door myself, but I can get into the building so much easier and more quickly when someone else opens it.

My Doorman

I like to think of Charlie as the most amazing "doorman" (or door-lady) I have ever known. Charlie has opened the door for my family to encounter doctors, teachers, therapists, parents, and even strangers in the grocery store who I may have never met otherwise. I can see these individuals simply as random people who have crossed our path over the years. Or I can see each person, each soul, as someone who needs a God encounter.

Perhaps God has known and designed, since before time began, for you and me to meet the parent whose child sits next to ours in class. Or the barista at the coffee shop who finds our child irresistibly precious. Can I challenge you to enlarge your perspective and see that God can accomplish His will on earth through the relationships and encounters He has designed for us and our children?

There are people all around us who are desperate to know the love of God, who need an invitation to church, who will be changed by an encouraging prayer, or who will be forever impacted by a bold testimony of God's work in our lives. I have found myself walking into each of these situations simply because Charlie opened the door.

Your child could open the door to a mother who has long forgotten that there is a God who loves her and has a plan for her life. She might have never received an invitation to church and you could lead her one step closer to discovering that God is pursuing her heart and wants to have a relationship with her.

Your child could open the door for you to encourage a friend who is also raising a child who might be "different." Because of your understanding and sympathy for the fears and struggles of mothering a child who doesn't fit the mold of others' expectations, you can bring strength and share the hope that the Lord has given you.

Your child could open the door to that doctor or therapist or teacher who has a broken marriage and home. As the love of Jesus shines through you and an inner strength permeates each conversation and interaction, you can have a meaningful connection or simply offer a genuine prayer that points them to a loving, heavenly Father.

If it wasn't for Charlie, I would never have crossed paths with so many people who need to know the love of Jesus. People I never would have met or interacted with are now contacts in my phone, play dates scheduled on my calendar, and names ever burning in my heart and in my prayers so they might know God and His love for them.

The Mission

We are all about mission trips in our home. We love to go to other nations—or across the country—and tell people about Christ. We have experienced some of our most powerful, faith-defining moments in the villages of Ghana, Africa, Lima, Peru, and the streets of New York City. It's amazing how a fourteen hour flight, a beastly line at customs, and a six hour bus ride can open my heart to a different culture, language, and way of life entirely.

But I also have a mission before me each and every day—and so do you. Every day we can open our eyes and hearts as our children open another door into someone's life. Another day with another opportunity to share the love of Christ. The door will be opened time and time again, but it is up to us to walk through it.

As you know, parents raising children with special needs often need encouragement. We get tired. We get discouraged. Some days, we just want to give up and call it quits. We need support. We need to know that we are not alone. We need someone to pick us up, dust us off, and tell us to keep going.

You and I are exactly the right people for that job!

Through the different encounters I've had with hurting and confused parents, God has made this mission clear to me. I have had countless, "random" conversations that I believe God orchestrated. I pray they have made an eternal impact. If it were just me, I could offer very little to a hurting parent raising a special-needs child. But because of God's truth and presence in my life, my story and my hope are able to encourage others.

There are times when I am not as bold on this mission as I should be. I have let some moments slip by because my mind was elsewhere, I lacked confidence, I didn't want to make others feel uncomfortable, or I let my own comfort trump the opportunity at hand. But for the moments when I let the Holy Spirit take the lead, and I lean into what He is doing in that moment, I see my purpose. I can hold onto Luke 21:15, "For I will give you the words and wisdom..." in those ministry encounters.

I can see my destiny arise as I put my life in His hands. He is the potter and we are the clay. Who are we to say how and when we should be used and for what purpose? (Romans 9:21). I want to be the hands and feet of Christ and I want my words to be the very words He has for those I meet.

Look for the Opportunities

How can we make a difference on the mission fields of our children's lives? Who can we talk to? How can we encourage others during those times when we are in a valley ourselves?

I believe it starts with prayer and seeking God's will and wisdom. Consider those the Lord has brought into your life who wouldn't be there if it wasn't for your "doorman." Your moments with that soul may be brief, so you must approach them with urgency in your heart and compassion to minister in whatever way the Spirit leads.

We can ask the Lord whom we should reach out to, chat with, or take out to enjoy a cup of coffee. Rather than a scheduled therapy session simply being about what new exercises our children can practice at home, we can initiate conversations about what the Lord has been doing in our lives, ask how we can pray for their needs, or tell them how grateful we are that the Lord blessed us with the help they give. *Lord, help us to have the boldness in these moments to shine for You and advance Your Kingdom!*

Shine in the Valley

Even when I am at my lowest points, in my deepest valleys, I have found that in the rawness of my pain and all my fears, God has set divine appointments to encourage a fellow mother who might be in a valley that feels an awful lot like mine. I don't have to put on a strong front to build her up. No—God is in my valley and God is in hers. I can shine the light of Jesus in her darkness even as it shines into the depths of mine. I can share my struggles, all the while pointing to the One who has pulled me out of every valley that lies behind me and who will reach down once again, pull me out, and set my feet on the Rock.

He lifted me out of the slimy pit, out of the mud and mire; he set my feet on a rock and gave me a firm place to stand.

—Psalm 40:2 (NIV)

We don't have to be walking in victory or a perfect circumstance to help others walk into theirs. We simply point to the One who leads us out of the valley and into His victory. God will choose when to use us and our children; we don't get to call the shots for when and where that might be. God will order our steps and lead the way. We simply need to be ready and willing to shine His light wherever and on whomever He might direct us.

Walk Through The Door

May the Lord give us boldness to walk through the doors He opens through our children! May we never grow numb to the opportunities at

God will choose when to use us and our children; we don't get to call the shots for when and where that might be.

hand, to the lives that can be set free by the message of the Gospel. As we go to the doctor and pray for healing and a good report for our child, let's also ask God for boldness to walk through the door and speak of what He has done in our lives!

Go Into All The World

As Christians, we are called to "go into all the world and preach the gospel" (Mark 16:15, NIV). We go into every man's world—the world of a fellow parent raising his or her special-needs child, the world of a doctor who has been in his practice for years but has never had a true God encounter, the world of teachers who love your child because they see something special on the inside but have yet to realize they're seeing the love of Christ.

I urge you to let your "doorman" open wide the doors of the ministry opportunities at hand daily! It is no accident that we are encountering these souls. We are part of God's plan for their lives. Let's be bold witnesses for Christ and the salvation He offers!

9
Then and Now

But Mary treasured up all these things and pondered them in her heart.
—Luke 2:19 (NIV)

Journals. I have them in boxes. I have them on shelves. I have them on my nightstand. They have gone with me around the world, tucked neatly in my carry on or safely in my suitcase. They have been filled with blue ink, black ink, pencil, even purple, or green ink. Some are filled with daily entries of faith and passion; others contain entries with dates spread over months. My faith journey can be best captured through these treasured journals.

Since the time I was young in my faith and personal relationship with Christ, I have reflected and prayed on page after page, in journal after journal. My life's stories fill these books. Pages with tear stains, smudged ink, and passion-etched dark lettering tell of my journey with the Lord.

When I look through the pages of my past, I often get pulled in, reading more than I planned. Some entries make me laugh at myself. How silly I was to be fearful in a situation where God carried me to victory. Or the words describing a conflict that seemed so major at the time, but when looking back, I've long-since completely forgotten about it. Reading these pages, I am amazed at the faithfulness God has demonstrated in every season and how He sustained me. I love to be reminded of what He spoke to me through His Word and in His presence—words that brought life and healing and strength to continue on.

Since I became pregnant with Charlie and now almost four years into motherhood, I have looked back at these pages to remind myself of all the stages of this journey that have brought us here today. I love to look back at the entries that tell of what God spoke to me, what He revealed through scripture, the conviction He brought to my spirit, and my heart's response along the way. I want to share just a few things God was doing *then* with you *now*.

Initially, when I planned on looking back, I thought today I would have truths from God I would have wished to have known four years ago. I planned to enlighten you (if you are at the beginning of your journey) with the experience I now carry.

However, the opposite has occurred. When I look back at the writings about our precious Charlie—the day we first saw red flags in the ultrasound, the day Charlie was born, the day we got the phone call about her diagnosis, the day God spoke to my heart that I was chosen to be her mother—I am amazed at the grace of God working in each moment of those days. I find strength and comfort as those pages remind me of what God did *then*. What He did *then* brings perspective and strength to my spirit *now*. So as I share with you, I pray that it does the same for you.

Where It Begins

The days after Charlie's blood test are all a blur while we were waiting for the report. Perhaps it was due to the little-to-no sleep that a mother gets after bringing home a newborn. It took everything in me just to shower each day, eat a balanced meal, and take those much needed moments to sit and be with the Lord and get into the Word. Several days had passed since we had received the call from the doctor letting us know that our daughter had Trisomy-21. I imagine that there were days that I couldn't face the Lord, not knowing what to say or how to say it. So days later, I stopped, I sat, I wrote. The entry below was written when Charlie was just eleven days old. It reveals a deep work that God was doing in my heart; a work that I hope never ends.

August 21, 2012

Lord, Your ways are higher than our ways. You have had a plan and good purpose for our lives since the beginning of time. Charlotte is the perfect gift to Luke and me—thank You. Thank You that You chose me to be her mom and Luke to be her dad. That's what You spoke to me this morning and that's what I am holding on to and standing on—Your word. Thank You for Your strength and peace and that You promise to be near, strong in our weaknesses, and that You have plans to give abundant life to Charlotte and us. God, again I thank You for a good thyroid, no leukemia, a good heart, good tone and strength in her arms and legs. God, if You will it, I believe You can heal her completely, but Lord, I also believe that You will give her the days, months, years, and life that You desire. God give us the healthiest baby girl possible—mentally, physically, emotionally and Lord, as more tests come in the future, give us strength and help us to have faith and peace. Draw Luke and me closer to You and to each other and Charlotte. The enemy will not steal our joy or our family. We belong to You. And You work all things together for the good of those who love You—that's us—we love You and You are doing a good work in us. Help me to be the mom Charlotte needs, the wife Luke needs, and surround us with faith and love-filled friends and family. Help us to know when and how to share this with friends. Pour into us, minister to our hearts, speak and let Your presence fill our home and our lives.

When I read this entry, I go back to these moments, lying on my bed, opening my heart up to the Lord. Throughout my life, God has been my safe place. I have run to Him time and time again and He is always there. He is truly my Comforter and Counselor (2 Corinthians 1:3-5, Isaiah 9:6).

He is there for us and ever-present and ready to help in our time of need (Psalm 46:1). He is our loving Father (John 16:27). Looking back and reading this prayer to the Lord, I see He was at work in me. He was surrounding me, sustaining me, and filling me so that I could not just crawl, not even walk, but run the race set before me.

On My Knees

From the beginning of this journey of raising a child with special needs, God has graciously drawn me to Himself. And I want to come on my knees in prayer—just as I am, in my hurt and pain, in my fears and failures, in my anger and frustration—and stay there with Him. For it is only in the Lord that we find strength to continue on. Just as I was on my knees back then, I want to always be on my knees now—seeking His face and interceding for my family. With Him I can be honest. I can be real. I can find rest. I can find wisdom. As parents, it starts on our knees and continues on our knees.

God never tires of us running to Him and kneeling at His feet. He never turns us away or wishes we would just get our act together and put on the "everything is fine" face. His arms are always open. My friend, run to the great Comforter. Let Him envelop you with His love. He will speak peace and life into your fear, pain, grief, anxiety—no valley is too deep for the Father to reach down to us, whom He dearly loves. He is a good Father, who lavishes His love on His sons and daughters.

God never tires of us running to Him and kneeling at His feet.

In this place, on my knees before the Father, I am amazed at the faith God gave me in that season. It's almost as if the words were not my own. Where did that strength come from? I feel like I am a broken mess half the time, but here, the Spirit of God had filled me with such hope. He helped me to keep my eyes on Him and not be overcome or fearful of the unknown.

Stand on the Word

I am amazed how the Lord graciously enabled me to hold onto His Word. In those moments, God gave me truth to stand on.

I will never leave you nor forsake you.

—Hebrews 13:5 (ESV)

(His) power is made perfect in weakness.

—2 Corinthians 12:9 (ESV)

I have come that (you) may have life, and have it to the full.

—John 10:10 (NIV)

All things work together for good to them that love God.

—Romans 8:28 (KJV)

He who began a good work in you will carry it on to completion until the day of Christ Jesus.

—Philippians 1:6 (NIV)

As His Word was stored up in my heart, it poured out in my prayers and in the pages of my journal.

As parents, we can be overcome with thoughts and fears that don't align with the truth of God and His will for our lives. We must read and/or listen to the Word, store it up in our hearts, put it to memory, and pray it over our children and our families. Life has a way of squeezing us (some seem to get squeezed more than others) and when it does, we may not always be proud of what comes out. I want the Word of God to shine in my darkness. I want His truth to silence any lies that may fill my thoughts. I want His promises to wash away any fears or doubts that may try to keep me from walking into everything God has for me as a mother, wife, and follower of Jesus.

Perhaps the Lord has already given you some scriptures to hold onto for your child, but if not, or if you are looking for a few more, I have some I would love to share with you.

These scriptures brought me strength and hope when Charlie was born. I wrote these verses down, posted them up on a simple cork board, and set them against Charlie's crib in her room. As I sat in her room each day, whether I was feeding her, changing her, rocking her, or playing with those sweet little feet, I had God's Word in plain view. These scripture verses encouraged my spirit and guarded my heart with truth.

I found them by simply starting to read in Psalms. As I read His Word, the Lord filled me each day. I took the time to read through these scriptures, and I challenge you afterwards to do the same. Keep His Word where you can see it. Read it daily, memorize it, and let it shape your prayers. You will find strength like you would not believe!

"The Lord will fulfill his purpose for me; your love, O Lord, endures forever—do not abandon the works of your hands."

—Psalm 138:8 (ESV)

"But you, Lord, are a shield around me, my glory, the One who lifts my head high. I call out to the Lord, and he answers me from his holy mountain. I lie down and sleep; I wake again, because the Lord sustains me."

—Psalm 3:3-5 (NIV)

"Know that the Lord has set apart the godly for himself; the Lord will hear when I call to him."

—Psalm 4:3 (NIV)

"You have put more joy in my heart than they have when their grain and wine abound."

—Psalm 4: 7 (ESV)

"The boundary lines have fallen for me in pleasant places; surely I have a delightful inheritance."

—Psalm 16: 6 (NIV)

"I keep my eyes always on the Lord. With him at my right hand, I will not be shaken. Therefore my heart is glad and my tongue rejoices; my body also will rest secure, because you will not abandon me to the realm of the dead, nor will you let your faithful one see decay."

—Psalm 16:8-10 (NIV)

"You, Lord, keep my lamp burning; my God turns my darkness into light. With your help I can advance against a troop; with my God I can scale a wall. As for God, his way is perfect: The Lord's word is flawless; he shields all who take refuge in him."

—Psalm 18:28-30 (NIV)

"I sought the Lord, and he answered me; he delivered me from all my fears. Those who look to him are radiant; their faces are never covered with shame."

—Psalm 34: 4-5 (NIV)

"… those who seek the Lord lack no good thing."

—Psalm 34:10 (NIV)

"The eyes of the Lord are on the righteous, and his ears are attentive to their cry…."

—Psalm 34:15 (NIV)

"I waited patiently for the Lord; he turned to me and heard my cry. He lifted me out of the slimy pit, out of the mud and mire; he set my feet on a rock and gave me a firm place to stand. He put a new song in my mouth, a hymn of praise to our God. Many will see and fear the Lord and put their trust in him."

—Psalm 40:1-3 (NIV)

Back then, I was startled at what a game changer it was to have His Word in front of me. God's Word is the light on our path and it makes each step sure and firm. His Word is true and never fails; not then and not now! We can forever hold onto God's Word as we raise our children. Only then can we have the strength we need and the perspective God desires for us!

Thankful Heart

When looking back, I am also challenged to be thankful in the moments of uncertainties. I knew nothing of the details of Charlotte's health, but I poured out thanksgiving to God, trusting that He would care for her. We, as parents, ought to give thanks in everything (1 Thessalonians 5:18). Yes, there may be bad reports and challenges for our children. But we can pray with faith and focus on the things God is doing and His goodness that still remains, in spite of the unexpected difficulties.

Do you remember those 3D-art images that were popular in the 1990s? They were computer generated and created quite a buzz. I remember staring at those things for what seemed like forever, trying to adjust my eyes just so, hoping the 3D image would pop out. Some people could look at those images and see the hidden picture within moments. But others grew tired and frustrated because they couldn't quite see and experience what they hoped.

It is the same with our lives. Some are able to look at life and pull out the positive; they seem to quickly identify and appreciate the art and handiwork of God. Others can never seem to quite see His good works. They aren't thankful because they can't see the good things that God is doing; they can't see the hidden picture.

As I ponder the work God was doing in my heart in those moments, I want to hold onto it and continue to allow Him to lead me to Himself. I want to be open and honest as I kneel before Him. And I want to stand on the truth and power of His Word. I know that as I stand on truth,

I can have the right perspective—see the picture that is sometimes hidden—and have a thankful heart as He continues to work in Charlie's life and in our family.

Identity

When you have a child with a disability, I believe it's important to watch out for the trap of mistaking the child's condition for his or her identity. In our attempt to guide and help our children through life, their disabilities can easily become something much greater than just a part of who they are. If we aren't careful, we can come to see the disability as our child's identity. Rather than seeing our son or our daughter as a whole person who is fearfully and wonderfully made by the Lord, we may begin to focus on and magnify the disability. And in the same way, the disability can become our identity as well. The diagnosis can become our entire universe—if we allow it.

The disability can be something our family journeys with and overcomes, or it can become something that defines us entirely. It can consume our every day, our every conversation, our every relationship so much that we can't remember life before we received the diagnosis. I remember a seasoned mother telling me to look past my daughter's almond-shaped eyes and simply see Charlie for herself. Much easier said

The disability can be something our family journeys with and overcomes, or it can become something that defines us entirely.

than done. In those early stages of processing her diagnosis, each time I looked at Charlie, my heart was heavy and saddened by the future ahead. The challenge was to see my daughter for who she was, not for what a blood test had labeled her to be.

God desires to work in every part of my life. That means I can't allow myself to be consumed by my daughter's disability or allow it to become the center of my existence. Charlotte's Down syndrome is not the only thing I talk to God about. I don't just read books on Downs research and the latest findings. Looking back at my journal entries, I see that the Holy Spirit is ever drawing me to Him and examining every part of my life.

April 24 (when the testing started)

I want to draw close to You, hear Your voice, and to be changed into Your likeness.

May 5

Draw us (Luke and me) closer to You—speak to Luke like only You can and bless him with Your presence.

June 4

I open my heart and life to You—search me and make me more like You. Even if it hurts and is embarrassing and uncomfortable, deal with me according to Your Word.

July 9

Lord, let me be the leader You want me to be. To submit to You, to serve my team, to be humble and patient, to love people the way You do, God. Mold and shape me for Your glory.

Don't Neglect Your Faith

Amidst all the ultrasounds and conversations with doctors and at home, God wanted me to give Him access to every area of my life. He was calling me to draw near to Him and have a deeper relationship with Him. He was leading me to pray for my husband. He was pulling things out of me to make me more like Christ. He was refining me as a leader in ministry. Though Charlie's health was a concern during this season, it was only part of what God was doing in my life. And the same is true today.

Just as Downs isn't Charlotte's identity or label, neither is being a "mother of a special-needs child" mine. All throughout this journey, as I pray for my daughter and hold onto God's Word, He is always working in me, sharpening my faith, drawing me into deeper intimacy with Him, and speaking to me about all areas of my life—even those that I haven't yet given fully to Him.

As I look back to when we first heard that Down syndrome was possibly going to be a part of our family, we gave it to God. We didn't let it become a god, or an idol; something that consumed us or was placed on the throne of our hearts to mold our thoughts or our decisions that would soon become who we are.

Though my journal is filled with intercession for Charlie, it is also filled with God speaking to me about my marriage, my thought life, my friendships, the ministry He has entrusted us with, and so much more.

Down syndrome doesn't define Charlie, nor does it define any part of our family. Whatever your child's disability, it should never become part of your identity. Yes, it is something you face, you pray about, and spend time and money on in order to help your child progress and overcome; but remember that there is more to life than that disability. Don't let it be bigger than it is. Let God, and nothing else, rule and reign in your life.

Even as I write those words of encouragement, I know it isn't easy to maintain a God-focused perspective amidst the trials you're facing. When such a great challenge is part of your daily life, it's easy for it to consume your conscious thought. Even now, there are times when I have to deliberately tell myself to stop talking about Charlie and her Down syndrome. I have to make myself talk to my husband about other things that happened throughout the day. I have to talk to my girlfriends about things other than Charlie's doctor appointments and latest medical expenses. I have to purposefully turn my mind to other things. Sure, I can talk about my daughter, but it doesn't and shouldn't always be about her disability. There is so much more to our children than a label that was given to them because of their disabilities. And through our conversation, we can either narrow others' focus to that label or let them see that there is much, much more to our child and our family than a disability.

Don't Neglect Your Family

Now, after having another child, I can see how Charlie's Downs could cause her ranking in the family to be higher simply because of her disability. I never want to neglect my son because our schedule, our conversation, our prayers, or our world seemingly revolve around Charlie. I want each of my children to feel individually loved and valued. I want to pray just as much for each of them that they would all experience God's power and love in their lives.

There is so much more to our children than a label that was given to them because of their disabilities.

More importantly, above my children, is my husband. We are designed to be one with our spouse, not with our children (Mark 10:8). I have to confess, there have been times when I have put Charlie above my husband. I need God's grace and wisdom to be the wife my husband needs and the one God has called me to be. We need to lean into our spouse first, and from our unity with one another will come greater love and strength in our home and for our children.

There are many statistics out there that point to higher divorce rates of those raising children who have special needs. But I like to think back to a simple bit of advice that has stuck with me; in order to be the best parent to your child, love your spouse. Wow, a parenting tip that is more of a marriage tip. But it makes sense. When we love our spouse, we provide security and stability for our children.

So in pondering these prayers, I am reminded that our identity is not in a diagnosis, but in the Lord. May God help us to be parents who never become consumed with worries about our children but who keep our hearts set on things above (Colossians 3:2).

Hold On

Let's never forget the precious promises and work of God in our hearts. I encourage you to write down your journey of faith and your prayers to the Lord. And as God speaks, don't be quick to forget His promises, but treasure them, and write them down as a way to store them up so that you, too, can look back and be reminded of the goodness of the Father. Let's continue to walk through our lives with the Lord, following as He leads the way, and holding on to the revelation He has already given.

10
Charlie's Angels

Therefore, since we are surrounded by such a great cloud of witnesses, let us throw off everything that hinders and the sin that so easily entangles. And let us run with perseverance the race marked out for us.
—Hebrews 12:1 (NIV)

The words that God tenderly spoke to my heart gave me the perspective that it is my privilege to mother such a beautiful gift. I believe that gift of being chosen to be part of Charlie's life extends beyond my husband and me as parents. In God's great design, He has chosen our family—her future siblings, each grandparent, aunt and uncle, cousin and relative—to be a part of Charlie's life.

And beyond our family, God has chosen those we love dearly—our friends, our church family—and those we simply love because Christ put them in our lives. Our neighbors, the employees at the grocery store I visit weekly (or even daily if I forget my list), and the barista who makes my coffee regularly but only recognizes me when I have a kid by my side. All those with whom Charlie has had a moment to connect and engage, whether brief or meaningful, have been chosen by God to be a part of her story, and she for theirs. I like to think of these individuals as the "angels" God has placed in our lives.

This truth is for you as well! You were chosen, your family was chosen, your friends were chosen, those you encounter have been chosen for your precious child!

God may use your child to reveal more of who He is, to open hearts that may have otherwise remained closed, and to bring a revelation that God so desperately desires to unfold. God will use our children to reveal who He is, to expose our own humanity and need for a Savior, and to lead us to walk with a greater grace and humility than we might otherwise.

Your son or daughter is a gift to this world, and the world will be marked by the fingerprints of your child. Our children were created for a purpose; and God will accomplish that purpose as we willingly give them into His hands and guide them to know the Father's will.

Ripple Effect

One of my favorite things to do as a kid was swimming. I practically lived in my best friend's pool every summer. In fact, many summers, my light blonde hair developed a hint of green due to overexposure to chlorine. We spent our time in the pool playing diving games, Marco Polo, tea parties at the shallow end, and one of my favorites—simple but endlessly entertaining—biggest splash contests. We would take turns jumping off the white diving board into the deep end, competing to see who could make the biggest wake in the water. We each had our signature jump which led to a great tidal wave that created endless ripples.

Merriam-Webster defines a *ripple effect* as "the spreading, pervasive, and usually unintentional effect" of a catalyst object. It doesn't take a giant leap into a pool to create ripples. A pebble tossed into a small puddle or even one simple touch on the water is all it takes to change the water's surface. Our children, our family, our testimony will naturally create ripples in the lives of those around us.

I love the story of Lazarus in the New Testament. How precious this man was to Jesus. Upon hearing of his death, we see a heart-felt sadness well up in Jesus that leads Him to tears (John 11:35). Jesus goes to the tomb of His dead friend and miraculously calls him out of it, bringing him back to life. Lazarus was transformed from death to life by the healing power of Jesus. He was forever changed, obviously!

But it wasn't only Lazarus' life that was changed. His resurrection must have created a ripple effect! Imagine how his sister, Mary, must

The world will be marked by the fingerprints of your child.

have been moved by this encounter. When I put myself in her shoes and imagine seeing a once-dead brother being brought back to life, I am convinced that my faith, my perspective on life, the way I treasure and treat my loved ones would forever be changed. Not to mention, it would radically increase my faith in Jesus!

Mary wasn't the only one affected. Others put their faith in Jesus once they heard of Lazarus' encounter with Christ (John 11:45). Jesus' work marked countless lives. And I believe the same is, and will be, true of our children. As God works in our children, in our families, the ripple effect will impact lives for eternity.

Breaking the News

One of the difficult obstacles Luke and I faced was how to tell others about our daughter's diagnosis. I remember the urgency we felt, not wanting to wait and avoid those conversations, but to get the report out as soon as possible. Though we were still dealing with the news ourselves, we figured others could start dealing with it—and praying about it—as well. The sooner we could share Charlie's diagnosis, the sooner we could move on to living our lives and adjusting to this new path the Lord had for us.

In a world of social media, news can travel faster than we want it to. It was important to us to share Charlie's diagnosis with our friends and family members personally, before they heard about it on Facebook. I remember calling dear friends and relaying the news.

From most of our friends, we received the same response. Whether over the phone, face to face, or even through email (one of my best friends was oversees doing mission work at the time), their responses mirrored one another. Each conversation ended with encouragement, love, support, and celebrating our new daughter just as if her diagnosis was that of a healthy baby girl. The friend I contacted through email responded with a note of hope and love:

She (Charlotte) is cherished already; I know this from your words and from the pictures. She is a true sweetheart and a bringer of great joy! Be encouraged that you do have Charlotte for a reason and that you were seen fit to be given her as a great gift. I want to hug you and kiss her!! I long to see you and Charlotte in three weeks when I fly in—I can't wait!

Her response to the news was encouraging and supportive. She may have had more questions and concerns, but for the time being, she focused on the positive and didn't seem to be shaken by the unexpected.

My hope is that you have a similar experience. It's wonderful to have friends and family quickly rally to give encouragement and love in your time of need. These individuals seem to easily accept your new normal and move forward with you.

If you have yet to hear it, my friend, let me be the first to encourage you. Your child is a gift, a beautiful gift that you have been entrusted with! I am excited for what the future holds for your family! God is going to carry you and do great things in your life and the life of your child! God has His hand on you.

But there are those even closer who may wrestle a little deeper, to be marked in an even more profound way.

Changed Forever

As parents, we can't help but be changed by our children. Their very presence in our lives enables us to better grasp the love of our heavenly Father and to glimpse another facet of His heart and thoughts towards us as we care for our little ones. The late nights and tears cried for our children drive us to understand the love God has for us as His children. Though underserved and surely not earned, we can't help but love our children and want the absolute best for them as we nurture and discipline them. And when given a child with special needs, I believe God tenderly reveals even more. God uses our children to teach us and those around us more than we could learn otherwise.

As the years have passed since Charlie's entrance into the world, our family continues the journey with God's plan and her place among us. I am more and more aware of how God has used Charlie to deepen my faith and relationship with Christ. I am not the same person I was four years ago.

Charlie has brought the perspective to our lives of what really matters. She has made me more compassionate and patient. She has marked my faith, teaching me how to pray with passion and sincerity. She has driven me to my knees time and time again to seek the Lord with a depth and earnestness I had never before experienced in my faith journey. God has used her to strengthen my marriage and bring our family closer together. The valley we traveled through as a family led us to a mountaintop of greater love for one another and hope for the future. I am who I am today because of my daughter.

God chose Charlie to mark not only my life but also my loved ones' lives in a profound way. My family is such a strong support system as we raise our children. With frequent plane rides and constant phone calls, I often share the ups and downs I am experiencing. As the weeks and months pass, we celebrate successes and breakthroughs for Charlie. I also continue to experience hurt and disappointment as a mother, and as

I share these feelings, my friends and family members share their heartbreak with me.

I wanted to share two letters with you: one from my older sister and one from my father. My sister and I were both pregnant at the same time——she with her second child and me with my first. Other than growing pregnant bellies at the time, we share a friendship and sisterhood that goes deeper than most sisters could experience. My daddy took me on my first date, shared with me his passion for music, and has been my biscuits and gravy breakfast date for as long as I can remember.

Along with our other family members, they both have been chosen for Charlie, and God has worked and continues to work deeply in their hearts. My hope is that as you read their words, your eyes are opened to the depth to which God can work in the lives of those closest to you, all because of the child He has chosen for you and your family.

God chose Charlie to mark not only my life but also my loved ones' lives in a profound way.

Dear Sister,

Our sister stars aligned when our pregnancies synchronized unexpectedly. It was pretty wonderful. We spoke across state lines and connected our pregnant hearts and bellies, our swollen bodies, aching feet, and funny husband stories. This unplanned blessing offered me hope after the complication with my first pregnancy, and I was eager to enjoy my second with my little sister who would help me walk confidently in the face of deeply buried fears.

We had inklings that something was different with Charlotte's progression, when routine ultrasounds showed us something was amiss with her measurements; my baby was huge, yours, small. You shared how doctors pulled you into offices, handed you pamphlets, and explained the possibilities of possible health concerns with Charlotte. Frustration filled my big-sister heart, imagining insensitive doctors using medical jargon to scare you into rethinking your pregnancy status and your future with your precious baby girl. I was so incredibly proud of you for stopping the doctors from testing for additional confirmation of their suspicions. You told them you were keeping her and you would not risk her life on a test. With each word you spoke during our check-ins, your confidence in God's provision and providence encouraged me to be brave with my own pregnancy. As I look back now, I see even then at the onset, you, my sweet sister, were my hero.

Charlotte surprised us that August night when we all received pictures of her little body resting on a newborn hospital bed, born to a strong and proud first-time mommy and daddy. My high-risk pregnancy kept me grounded here, sadly distant from your delivery and first few moments home, but mom was able to come to you right away. I was anxious because I wanted to be with you and help you with the new mommy bomb that explodes your life, changing everything in ways only mommies understand. As your big sister, it was my job to help you and I was also anxious to protect you from the additional stress coming at you from the medical world. Within moments of Charlie's birth, tests were needed and being run to confirm "stuff." I intentionally use the word "stuff" because to me, it didn't matter what anyone said, doctors or nurses or bloodwork. I treasured those first pictures of Charlotte on my phone and looked at them constantly. I wasn't looking for clues to a diagnosis; I was looking for Charlie, for you, for Luke, for Jesus. I kept looking and wondering what the tests would say. Then I wondered what our family would collectively and independently say right back to the tests.

A few days after Charlotte was home, mom called, crying.

We talked about how hard it is as daughters to know what to do with our momma when she cries because she is the perfect practical mixture of solid and sweet. This was no exception and hearing her was agonizing. Mom said the tests came back. Trisomy-21. Charlotte Joy had Down syndrome. I knew then once she said it out loud that our lives would change forever. My memories are cloudy from there. Mom said you and Luke were on a walk, and she was taking care of Charlie. I told her to be there for you, to provide the peace and strength and support like only she could. I told mom to be strong. I told her she could process it later when she returned home. Since I could not be there for you, I wanted mom to be my stand-in. The last thing I told her was, "Be strong, mom. Be strong."

My mind and heart overflowed with feelings of powerlessness, fear, and confusion. I felt I had no right to feel anything because I was standing on the outside and feeling my way along. I didn't want to intrude on you and Luke by flipping into big protective sister mode, so I walked gently, spoke little, and tried to listen more than anything. You and I talked shortly after I talked with mom. I don't remember any specific moment, more a collection of moments stretching out time and the distance between us. Charlie and you felt so far away, with so many unknowns and what ifs out of my control. I imagined you making tough phone calls and changing endless diapers, and trying to establish a new normal in all of the mess which made my heart ache. I didn't know what to do. We talked. We sat quietly. We prayed. With words, silence, and tears, we leaned into our sisterhood because I knew deep in my core that you, sweet sister, would not just be my hero but our family's hero, too.

Sister, I am here for you. I won't always know what to say or ask or do, but I know God has asked me to be your champion. To hold you up in prayer, encourage you, and connect like we always have. I want to be there as we both figure out how to be moms to our kids and aunts to our nieces and nephews. I want to create a little bit of normal for us.

You can expect me to be praying, always praying. I will listen and not offer advice even if I want to. I may make mistakes, ask the wrong questions, and make assumptions. Know you can come to me with the good, the bad, and the in-between in our sisterhood friendship. Being a mom is rough and I love you. I may not always be able to relate, but I will always be able to pray and listen and hope.

I know there are many challenges ahead. I am here for you to pray with you, offer input, or just grovel with you when life happens. Taking care of Charlie is my concern, too. I want you to know my family is privileged to help as we can. It's our opportunity to participate in raising and taking care of our precious niece. When you share your concerns and express needs, it connects our families and teaches us all how to better love and care for each other. You show me with each passing challenge how true strength is interwoven with dependency on Jesus Christ and Scripture, and being a hero is about being human and reaching out to others in strength and weakness.

The unknowns to come are daunting for all of us because life is complicated and our children are growing up in a changing world. You can count on me to help Charlie be the best woman of God she can be, to walk boldly, to love richly, to believe courageously. My heart floods with anticipation as I imagine her taking hold of her identity in God. I am honored to stand behind her, unashamedly cheering her on as she changes the world. I am also here to help you be the best mom you can be, the mom Charlie needs. I am here to do whatever I can to help you because you, my sweet sister, are Charlie's hero, too.

I want you to know that you were made for this adventure, and there is no one in the entire universe better chosen for Charlie.

I love you more than words,

Jamie

Dear Jennifer,

Looking back at how this all began, I recognize now how absolutely unprepared I was for the arrival of the gift of Charlotte Joy and how I need to acknowledge that to you and thank you for your remarkable graciousness to all of us through this unexpected and extremely challenging experience.

The clues about Charlotte's health filtering through the family chatter, including the doctor's prenatal concerns, somehow did not register. Or perhaps, I did not allow them to register. Every time your mother or sister would mention something about the possibility of health issues, I automatically dismissed them with my highly developed defense and denial system. There was no chance of problems with Jen's baby, I thought; there have never been any problems like this with the babies in our family.

I remember the exact moment I knew something was exceptional about this child. The pictures of the newest member of our family came with all the excitement and deep emotion of this momentous event. In her proud father's arms, I saw our newest granddaughter and was silenced by the appearance of a few unusual features. Could it be? Something exceptional about this child that would forever change us: how we saw our family and the world, even God Himself? In typical fashion, I analyzed facts and rationalizations that would convince me everything could be explained, facts and information I could share with my family, especially you, precious daughter, that would give some comfort and ensure all was OK.

Before my lonely and lengthy journey to Detroit to join your new family and your mother, my pondering nearly spiraled into despair. I remember going through memories of any of my family's physical characteristics for evidence of some similar characteristics to our new granddaughter. I kept falling back with the imagination that someone in her father's family must have features just like hers. As my internet search continued, it drew me into an increasing agony of fear and turmoil until I realized I had to take hold of my mind and call on God for His grace and strength to face what was now becoming far too real. How could I be so weak and unprepared for this unusual but predictable happening in our family? Surely others-by now I realized there were many others-had faced this issue before and somehow come through.

As I arrived, I soon realized God had already masterfully prepared the answer to my prayer. It wasn't just peace of mind that I needed. It was a whole new perspective, a whole new way of understanding our lives, and what was important. The breakthrough began when I entered your home and felt the overwhelming love and nurture for my new granddaughter within. I knew it was enough. When you handed her to me, the feel of her warmth brought a profound and unexplainable comfort to my weary soul. She was my granddaughter, and I knew she belonged to our family and to me in a divinely good way. Seeing the genuine love and care Luke, your mother, and you had for her eliminated the uncertainties that had so unnecessarily troubled me.

In the days ahead, everything aligned to form a perfect perspective and meaning regarding the coming and appreciation of Charlotte Joy. Three things in particular hit me. My children: how ironic that God showed me what I could not perceive through my children. The first was a casual comment from my son, Daniel, who had some experience of teaching children with disabilities. As he learned about Charlotte's special nature, he simply said, "This will be good for our family because she will teach us things we would never otherwise know." The second came from your sister, pregnant herself, whose reaction to knowing what her baby sister must be going through reflected, "I'm so concerned for her. I would trade places with her in a heartbeat if I could." Hence, the power and wonder of unconditional love was revealed.

But you settled the matter and laid a foundation for a life in our family's future in a surprising and magnificent breakthrough of wisdom and grace. About a week after Charlotte's birth, I now know you called me with nothing short of a divine revelation. You simply shared what happened when God unexpectedly visited you and set your soul straight. Your words, as I remember them, were clear and matter of fact, "Dad, I was in the shower and God showed me what this was all about. He had chosen us to raise a child He had brought into this world for a very special purpose. So I prayed that God would help me be the best mother I could be to help Charlotte to become all that God planned for her to become and do." That was the final word and the truth of where we all would stand. There was nothing more to be said, so I too prayed to God to help me become the best grandfather I could be to this special child to help her in fulfilling His special purpose for her life. Where I had fallen short with this unfathomable change of circumstances, you, my daughter, had heard from God and were now able to lead us all into the kingdom with hope and purpose for our new assignment.

With much love and pride in you and my new granddaughter,

Dad

Cloud of Witnesses

We, as parents, are not the only ones being impacted by our children. Our children are marking those around us. God is using Charlie to impact the faith, the family dynamic, the very core of each member of our family. If I could include a letter from each member of our family, they would have a story to share of how God is working and transforming them in a way they never expected.

I believe the same is true in your life. God is using your child to advance His kingdom in the midst of your life and the lives of others, especially your family. You may have the privilege of hearing their stories, their testimonies, or you may never know the dealings of the Lord in their hearts and minds; either way, know that they are watching and they are impacted greatly.

I understand that some families have difficulty accepting a family member with a disability. I have heard stories of grandparents neglecting their granddaughter or grandson and refusing to open their hearts to a child that has special needs. My heart breaks for these families. I can't imagine how anyone would not open his or her heart to such a beautiful, precious child. I pray your experience is that you have a very supportive family who loves and embraces your child just as just as he or she is.

The angels who surround your child are impacted. God uses the foolish things of this world to teach the wise (1 Corinthians 1:27). It's the unexpected encounters that can mark others the most. God is using our testimonies and our precious children in ways we may never know.

To The Chosen

So to those who are chosen, just as I am, let's keep our eyes fixed on the Author and Perfector of our faith and walk boldly knowing that we have been set apart for our precious children (Hebrews 12:2, Psalm 4:3).

By the goodness of God, we have the honor of seeing His glory revealed and of leading our children into the fullness of knowing Christ and His love for them. We get to journey through this life with our spouse and loved ones and see the power of prayer unfold in every season. We get to dig ditches for our children and see lives forever impacted as our children open doors for us on a mission path we may never have otherwise encountered. And we get to experience the goodness of God, for He never changes. Throughout this path that lies ahead, others are being just as marked and moved by God's work in our children as we are. May our gift be for His glory. Thank you, Lord, that we are chosen for our children!

Acknowledgments

To my husband, Lucas, who has taken every step of this journey with me: at times you have been by my side, other times you have led me, and even carried me. You are an incredible husband, loving father, and God's amazing gift to me.

To my family, who have loved and supported Lucas and me as we parent and in writing this book: You bring strength, encouragement, and joy to our lives. Thank you for standing with us, praying with us, and celebrating God's goodness in our lives. Your prayers, wisdom, and encouragement carried this book, and for that, I am grateful.

To Sue Detweiler, who has mentored me as an author and woman of God: Thank you for teaching me, praying with me, and helping me to turn this book from words on my computer into an effective platform to share a God-inspired message with others. I am so grateful for all you invested in me and for challenging me to run fast and hard, while being led by the Spirit.

To Erin Casey and her team, whose talent and excellence have made this book something I am so proud to share: Thank you for all the time given to refine, polish, and present this message to be as effective and impacting as possible.

To my church family at Cornerstone Church: You have surrounded our family and brought strength to our souls. I am so grateful for the way you have embraced and celebrated our Charlotte Joy. Thank you for every smile, every hug, every high-five, every bit of love you have shown to our daughter.

To my fellow mommas raising little ones with special needs: You have each been sent specifically and strategically by the Lord—whether you mentored me, prayed with me, gave me advice, exchanged the ups and downs of parenting—you know who you are. And to the mommas I am yet to meet who will continue to shape me and teach me: I am honored to walk this path with you.

To all our family and friends who have encouraged, prayed for, and financially given to help publish this book: To you, I am so grateful and beyond blessed that you would surround us in such a powerful way.

To my Charlotte Joy, my daughter, my dance partner, my sing-along buddy, my little woman: You have taught me more about myself, forever marked my faith, and shown me Jesus. Your smile lights up a room and your joy is contagious. Your daddy and I are your biggest fans; we love you, believe in you, and can't wait to see all that God has in store for you.

To my Savior, Jesus, who is my joy, my strength, my source of life: You pulled me out of a pit of despair and you sustain me daily. You are my Anchor and the Rock on which I stand. You have spoken so powerfully and graciously that I have to share it with others. I pray You take this book and bring the same healing and breakthrough that you have brought me. May every chapter, scripture, and word shared be a testimony of Your goodness. You are the answer, You are the hope, You are my everything.

About the Author

Jen Forsthoff's experience in raising her daughter with Down syndrome and her ability to communicate biblical truths, which apply to parents gifted with a special-needs child, brings life and hope to readers as she shares her testimony in an honest and authentic manner. She strives to bring spiritual breakthrough and victory for every parent, grandparent, and individual entrusted with a special-needs child.

Her Calling

Jen is a mother of two, pastor's wife, worship leader, and writer. She serves faithfully in her local church and has committed herself to the call of God in her life. As an Oral Roberts University graduate with a degree in Elementary Education, her experience in the classroom, among young families, and in ministry has given her both the experience and education that enables her to effectively communicate a meaningful and life-giving message. Jen longs for others to embrace the calling to parent his or her child specifically gifted to him or her and fulfill that calling with faith and total reliance on God and His Word.

Chosen and Gifted

When Jen and her husband, Lucas, began to plan their family years ago, she never imagined having a child with Down syndrome. Though doctors had initial concerns during her pregnancy, she refused testing, believing that regardless of the diagnosis, God was in control. A beautiful baby girl was born and later the doctor's suspicions were confirmed. Charlotte, her sweet baby Charlie girl, had Trisomy-21.

When the fear became a reality, she turned to God, seeking answers and desperate for something to hold onto. Then God spoke,

"I chose you to be her mom."

In a moment, the healing began. Fear and heaviness was replaced with joy and privilege. Jen received this word from the Lord and hasn't turned back. Once embracing her calling that she was chosen for Charlie, Jen has found healing, inspiration, and power through the word of God in every season.

Rising Up and Speaking Out

It is now her burden and honor to share this message with other mothers, parents, grandparents, and anyone who has been chosen to love and care for a special-needs child. While experiencing true victory and breakthrough, she has chosen to rise up and speak out. No matter the severity or confirmation of the diagnosis, Jen wants to bring hope and strength to others, as she shares from her personal journey as a young mother. She also hopes to impart the power of God's Word and how it applies to every parent on a similar journey.

Jenforsthoff.com

Jen@jenforsthoff.com

#chosenforcharlie

CPSIA information can be obtained
at www.ICGtesting.com
Printed in the USA
FSOW04n2305270416
19763FS